Praise for *Skunk Train*

"Here a teenager on a mission endures and enacts all manner of crime. The road to becoming a man is not just rocky for Kyle, it is filled with figurative craters, sinkholes, and mountains. Buckle up and hold on tight. It's a fast and rough road trip you won't want to miss."

—Jeffery Hess, author of *No Salvation*

"Three are dead at the Skunk Train Inn and 15-year-old Kyle Gill is on the run with a bag of cash—hunted by a small-time dealer, crooked cops, and a Mexican cartel. A heart-pounding thriller which could be dubbed 'no country for *young* men'."

—J.L. Abramo, Shamus Award-winning
author of *Gravesend*

"Gritty, raw and rough-edged, but with perceptive observations about life and a tender heart at its center. It's so good every time I had to stop reading I couldn't wait to get back to it to find out what was happening to Kyle and his girlfriend Lizzie. Tense, terse and fast paced—a must read."

—Paul D. Marks, Shamus Award-winning
author of *White Heat*

SKUNK TRAIN

ALSO BY JOE CLIFFORD

Stand Alones
Wake the Undertaker
The One That Got Away

The Jay Porter Series
Lamentation
December Boys
Give Up the Dead
Broken Ground
Rag and Bone

Memoir
Junkie Love

Short Story Collections
Choice Cuts

As Editor
Trouble in the Heartland:
Crime Fiction Inspired by the Songs of Bruce Springsteen

Just to Watch Them Die:
Crime Fiction Inspired by the Songs of Johnny Cash

As Co-Editor
Hard Sentences:
Crime Fiction Inspired by Alcatraz

JOE CLIFFORD

SKUNK
TRAIN

TUFTS LIBRARY
WEYMOUTH, MA

Copyright © 2019 by Joe Clifford

All rights reserved. No part of the book may be reproduced in any form or by any electronic or mechanical means, including information storage and retrieval systems, without permission in writing from the publisher, except by a reviewer who may quote brief passages in a review.

Down & Out Books
3959 Van Dyke Road, Suite 265
Lutz, FL 33558
DownAndOutBooks.com

The characters and events in this book are fictitious. Any similarity to real persons, living or dead, is coincidental and not intended by the author.

Cover design by Zach McCain

ISBN: 1-64396-055-5
ISBN-13: 978-1-64396-055-5

JAN 2 4 2020

The book is dedicated to my baby sister, Melissa.
It's just the two of us now, kiddo.

Northern California,
sometime around 2010…

CHAPTER ONE

Kyle saw the opened school envelope on the counter as soon as he stepped inside the trailer. He wasn't surprised. Once Ronnie said Deke was looking for him, he knew he was in trouble. The only time his cousin ever looked for him was when he was in trouble, which seemed to be more and more of late. Fist fights. Meetings with counselors. Write-ups and detentions. Since he stopped going to school, Kyle had been smart enough to sneak back to the trailer and get the mail before Deke did. Today he'd gotten distracted, too stoned on the Highway. Of course the first day he missed the mailman, the letter would come. Just his luck.

For the past three weeks Kyle had left the trailer every morning like he was going to school. Didn't matter if Deke was already gone for the day or that neighbors up here didn't talk to each other, the little shacks and sheds buried among the Northern California redwoods spread too far apart to invite much company. Kyle wanted to keep up the routine. Wake up, brush teeth, eat cereal, put back the milk. Then he'd disappear into the woods to pedal his old bicycle down to the Highway. Sell a dime bag from Deke's stash at the Ironside, the biker bar up the road, hang with the older skater dudes behind the strip mall, wait till Ronnie got home from class. Kyle knew everyone would blame his recent behavior on the pot. But pot really had nothing to do with it. Up in Humboldt County everyone started smoking the stuff. Eventually. And smoking wasn't the cause of his problems—smoking was the result of his problems, a way to cope—he remembered that from an assembly last fall. The truth was something inside him had broken. Just short of his sixteenth birthday, Kyle couldn't explain what that something was, not to teachers or Ronnie, certainly not Deke. Kyle's life had been rough since his dad dropped him off on his cousin's doorstep. Kyle had always been moody; at least that's what Deke called it. If having two emotions—sad and angry—constituted moody. If Kyle didn't say anything, kept his head down, he could withdraw deep into himself. Survive the day. Which was the better of the two options. Because anytime he tried to express himself, these feelings he had, it ended bad. Pushed hard enough, he'd lash out. Because Kyle wasn't a big kid, that usually ended up with his ass kicked. But he wasn't chickenshit or scared to throw a punch. That's the one thing living with Deke had taught him. Better to get pounded than be thought a coward.

No one was inside the trailer, but Kyle could hear Deke and Jimmy, his business partner, arguing out back. The trailer wasn't actually a trailer—that's what Kyle called it because it was so small. He'd lived there since he was five. It's hard to remember much at that age, memories just out of reach, like the details of a dream you've already forgotten upon awaking. He knew he missed his mom a lot, and that he cried when his dad dropped him off following the funeral service because he'd wanted live with his father in Hollywood. But his dad was too busy making movies.

Through the kitchen window, he spied them by the toolshed. Kyle couldn't make out what they were saying, but Deke and Jimmy were going at it pretty hard, in each other's face, jabbing fingers, standing toe to toe. Deke was sucking on that Marlboro Red like a fiend. Kyle liked Jimmy, who rented a booth at Blood and Bones, the tattoo parlor on the Highway. He was certainly cooler than Deke.

Kyle already regretted cutting class, knew it was going to bite him on the ass. In truth, Kyle was bored shitless, and most of the time he wished he were back at school. But too much time had passed to walk back into class now. He had to wait for this to play out. Thanks to that letter, he wouldn't have to wait long.

Kyle brushed aside the rest of the mail, utility, gas—but not cable because Deke was too cheap to spring for that—shopping flyers, the empty takeout containers. He searched for a cigarette in an ashtray but couldn't find one. Foggy, gray light crept through the threadbare curtains, these cheesy things with dangling, frilly dice that Kristy, Deke's ex, had picked up at a consignment shop when they'd all gone for breakfast in Cutting. That was a nice morning. He missed having Kristy around. At least she *tried* to talk to Kyle once in a while.

Kyle chugged the half can of warm Mountain Dew, and stared into the dense, green thicket of Mendocino Forest. Dark clouds churned in the distance, upturning leaves on the trees, thunderstorm brewing.

Let's do this. With Jimmy there, Deke was less likely to lose his shit.

Kyle shoved open the screen door, and both Deke and Jimmy jumped out of their boots. Everyone in Dormundt knew those two didn't take shit from anyone. Kyle felt good that he'd scared them.

Deke whipped the letter from his back pocket, waving it around, eyes squinty mean. He pointed a finger at Kyle. "Stay right there."

"I ain't going anywhere." Kyle nodded at Jimmy. "What's up?"

"How's it hanging, little man?"

"Go back inside," Deke said.

"You told me not to go anywhere."

"Don't be a smartass."

Kyle smoldered in place, trying to look tough.

"Go!"

Kyle yanked open the screen door, flinging it wide and letting it slam. He stalked near the window, trying to keep his edge. Now that they knew he was home, they were talking quieter.

Like Kyle cared about whatever lame secret Deke had.

Soon as Deke came inside, Kyle was telling him. He had made up his mind. He was moving to L.A. to live with his dad. He'd threatened it before but this time he would follow through. He imagined Deke getting all teary-eyed when he saw Kyle wasn't playing around, and then his cousin would calm right down, try to backpedal, say Kyle couldn't leave, how much he needed him, but Kyle would tell him too bad, he was out of there, no matter how much his cousin begged him not to go. Kyle would grab his stuff, all stone-cold and silent, and head out, leaving behind a weepy Deke to wonder why he had to be such a dick.

And that's where the fantasy dried up.

Because Kyle couldn't get on his bicycle and pedal five hundred miles to L.A., or even the twenty to the Greyhound station in Richter. Plus, he had *no* idea where his dad lived, and studios have security guards. He didn't even have the same last name as his dad. No one would believe him. No one believes anything when you're fifteen.

Kyle sat down at the kitchen table in the dimming light, peeling labels off empty beer bottles, wadding spitballs and flicking them with his thumb. He must've dozed off because he woke up still sitting at the table but now it was dark.

He heard Jimmy's truck fire up, and Kyle steeled his resolve for the fight with his cousin. But when Deke walked in all he did was pace back and forth, pulling aside the dice curtains, gazing out the window and watching taillights disappear. He fired up another smoke even though he still had one in his mouth.

It was getting late, darker, but no one bothered to turn on any lights. Something had Deke rattled, and it was more than Kyle's cutting class. Deke hadn't said one word to him, pacing, chain-smoking, staring down the black country road long after Jimmy's truck was gone.

"What's wrong?" Kyle asked.

Deke snapped to and pulled the letter from his back pocket,

holding it up, before slapping it down on the counter. "Like I don't have enough shit to worry about, you have to pull this stunt?"

"It's not a stunt."

"You're going back. You hear me? Tomorrow."

"Tomorrow's Saturday."

"Don't be a smartass."

Kyle wanted to say like hell he was, dig in his heels and make a stand, but something wasn't right. Deke had resumed pacing, acting a nervous wreck. Kyle didn't like this, Deke losing his cool. Kyle hated Deke most of the time, hated him for always giving him a hard time, for being a loser, for not being somebody important like his dad, but Kyle also respected how tough he was. He'd once seen Deke almost break a man's arm in two for trying to rip him off. A couple winters back, this skeezy junkie, Chip Morsman, came by the trailer with two jacked-up buddies. Chip had bought a pair of tires off Deke, then tried to weasel out of paying because he said the tread on one of them was worn, which was a lie since Chip had picked out the tires himself. Chip must've figured with his two buddies there, both tatted and built like farm oxen, Deke wouldn't start any trouble. But he didn't know his cousin. Deke picked up an ax handle—just the wood part and not the actual blade—and he cracked Chip so hard in the eye you could hear the bone splinter across the yard. Then he wrapped the handle behind Chip's arm, twisting it and lifting him off the ground until Chip cried like a baby and made his buddies grab his wallet and pay Deke. His cousin was a lot of things, but he wasn't chickenshit. Right now, though, Deke looked terrified, and that terrified Kyle.

Then his cousin did something unexpected. He came over and wrapped his arms around Kyle, hugged him tight. Deke never did that. Kyle didn't know how to respond, so he sat there, body tensed, trying not to cry. Kyle had spent the last three weeks gearing up for a big showdown, but this wasn't playing out like he'd imagined.

"Come on," Deke said, walking out back.

Night had fallen hard, the sky over Spy Rock stained mud gray, and a harsh cold wind blew in from the Pacific and over the Ranges, rustling the forest. Deke pulled out a joint and sparked it. He took a hit and passed it to Kyle, who looked up, unsure what to do.

"Yeah, I know you smoke. What'd'ya think? I'm stupid?"

Kyle took the peace offering.

"And I know you take money out of my dresser, and I know you pinch my stash and go down the strip mall and sell to those hoodrat turds." Deke shook his head. "I never asked to be your dad. I didn't have a choice."

Kyle didn't know what to say.

"Your father couldn't take care of you after your mom died. He's not that kind of a guy. It's not only 'cause he's an asshole. He don't have a caring bone in his whole rotten body."

Deke didn't talk much about his father anymore. Any time Kyle brought him up, it ended in a blowout. Kyle didn't want to say anything, hoping maybe his cousin would keep talking. But he stopped.

Deke took a couple steps into the tall backyard weeds, before turning around. "I need you to stay at Ronnie's for a few days. I ain't mad at you. But you have to go there. Okay? For a little while."

"I can't. Ronnie's mother hates me."

"Shit, man, ain't there *any*where you can go?"

"Maybe I can stay with my dad." Kyle was trying to be helpful but that was the wrong thing to say.

"Don't you think if I knew how to find the sonofabitch I'd have called him by now?"

"You're just saying that because you're jealous."

"Why would I be jealous of that asshole?"

"Because he's down in Hollywood, making movies, and you're a loser working in a bar, dealing dope." Kyle didn't feel bad for Deke anymore.

"Oh, yeah? If he's such a great guy, how come he ain't never called you? Doesn't write you no more?"

"You probably told him not to."

"No, Kyle. Your father ain't called, and he don't write, because he's a selfish prick. He didn't want you to live with him. That's why he dumped you here."

Kyle leapt at his cousin, a half punch, part shove. Deke ducked out of the way and Kyle stumbled to his knees.

"I hate you," Kyle spat from the ground.

"Pack some clothes."

"Screw you."

"I'm not kidding. We need to get out of here."

"I'm not going anywhere with you."

Deke grabbed Kyle by the arm, dragging him to the toolshed, Kyle resisting the whole way, until his cousin flipped him over and Kyle tumbled into the weeds. Deke pulled the wad of keys off his belt and opened the lock. He tugged the string and a dangling bulb blazed bright.

On the floor of the old toolshed lay two large canvas bags. Deke knelt down and unzipped them. Marijuana. Lots of it. Sealed in plastic wrap, stacked high and deep, front to back.

Deke never carried more than a sandwich baggie or two.

"How much is here?"

"I don't know."

Kyle tugged one of the handles. The bag didn't budge. "Are you nuts? You can't leave this out here. This shed's falling apart. Anyone could come bust that lock with a rock. We've got to bring it in the house."

"We can't bring it in the house."

"Why not?"

"Because that's the first place they're gonna look."

"Who?"

"Who do you think? The people we stole it from."

CHAPTER TWO

The plan had been to meet up for breakfast at the Log Cabin earlier that day, the roadside diner along 37, talk about expanding operations, before heading out to Bodhi's place. But Deke had gotten hung up stripping scrap in Eureka, leaving Jimmy to drink coffee at the counter, alone. Jimmy wasn't going to bust his balls. He knew Deke had his hands full with that little shit, Kyle. Jimmy had been seeing Kyle down on the Highway for weeks, peddling dimes at the Ironside, getting stoned behind the old video store. Jimmy tried to ring Bodhi to say they were running late but couldn't get through. Which was normal. No cell reception where Bodhi lived, and the paranoid fucker wouldn't install a landline, worried cops would tape his conversations. Jimmy was anxious to move. Word had drifted down about the big bust a few nights earlier, a large shipment of grass impounded between Cutting and Richter, the third seizure in the past couple months, which would dry the pipeline and make prices soar. Tough shit for them. But a potential good turn for Jimmy and Deke. Gotta love a seller's market when you're the one holding.

When Deke got there, they left his truck at the diner and took Jimmy's Ford F-150. Bodhi lived on a trailer compound in the middle of nowhere, a layout ripped straight from *Mad Max* or one of those reality shows about hillbillies hoarding canned goods, waiting for the apocalypse. Like so many places in the Humboldt wilds, there were no street signs to tell you where you were going. Because no one up here wanted to be found.

It's why people lived here in the first place. You'd have to look for markers, burned stumps or washed-out bridges, the old horse bones by the collapsed barn, welcome to Hicksville.

The region's cool mountain climate provided the perfect environment for growing, and the dense cover made it impossible for the authorities to zero in. Most of the time the cops didn't give a shit. New measures got introduced on the ballot every fall to get around federal law and make growing legit. But even after Prop 215 passed, which let farmers harvest a certain number of plants for medicinal use, Jimmy doubted it'd ever be straight-up legal. Too much money in keeping it the other way. Payoffs. Kickbacks. And don't forget the Mexicans, who'd never let marijuana be taxed and regulated like produce. The fresh crop of politicians who rode in every year, promising to preserve tradi-tional family values, were beating the same "Just Say No" dead horse from when Jimmy was a kid. The bastards brokered back-room deals with the Mexicans all the time. They were all crooks. No problem ever got solved by pulling a lever or punching a ticket. A good hard kick to the teeth got your point across much quicker.

For several years now, Deke and Jimmy had been buying from Bodhi, who violated stereotypes of the old, peaceful, hippy pot farmer. Yeah, Bodhi had two young wives, whom he referred to as "sisters," and a pack of half-naked, filthy kids could always be found prowling the grounds, shrieking posters for birth con-trol. Bodhi also stockpiled semi-automatics and assault rifles, getting ready for the inevitable all-out war with the government. Jimmy nicknamed the place Waco.

Jimmy found the fire-scarred tree, and turned up the dirt road, a narrow passage of tamped-down thicket and thorn. Sitka branches brushed the windshield like an automatic carwash, and the musky scent of huckleberry ribboned through the truck's vents.

"Ran into Kristy the other day," Jimmy said, keeping his F-150 at a steady fifteen. Couldn't go any faster than that or you'd drop the transmission in the potholes.

"So?" Deke lit a cigarette.

"She was asking about you."

"She knows where to find me."

"Hand me that." Jimmy reached for the lighter Deke had stuck back on the dash. "Ain't none of my business, man. But I don't see you tapping anything else in Dormundt."

"It's not that simple."

"Nothing is. Figured you could use the extra hand with Kyle, is all. She likes him, don't she?"

"That's the problem. This is shit you don't have to worry about."

"I'm almost thirty. I ain't any younger than you."

"That's not what I mean," Deke said. "It ain't about being a kid. It's about having to take care of one."

"Kyle ain't yours. Man, you've already done more for that little shit than anyone could've asked for. You feed him. Clothe him. Pay for his dentist. What the fuck for?"

"He's family."

"Fuck family."

"He's had it rough."

"Who hasn't?"

"Boys like Kyle," Deke said, "you got to be careful who you introduce into their lives. His mom died real early, his dad's a shit. He's going to latch on to other people to fill those roles."

"Sounds like something you read in a parenting book."

"Maybe it is. What else can I do?"

"Take care of *numero uno*, that's what. I see punks like him on the Highway all day long. That boy is a lost cause. You're pissing your life away on him." Jimmy took a drag, swiveling his head to get a better look through the trees. "Something ain't right with that kid."

"He's got no street smarts."

"He lives in Dormundt. What the hell's he need street smarts for?"

* * *

They entered a clearing and the grounds came into view, four trailers in the shape of a diamond, a feng shui design that Bodhi said allowed the nurturing energy of the Earth Mother to flow uninterrupted. Deke noted the new, bigger artillery shed, repositioned off to the side. Barefoot boys and girls, long, stringy hair and faces caked with mud, ran around without shirts. Tall redwoods climbed the steep hillside, their unseen tips spearing the fog and disappearing into heaven's descent.

An old Dodge Dart Deke didn't recognize jammed up the ass of Bodhi's 4x4, blocking him in.

"Bodhi get a new truck?"

Jimmy shrugged, then reached over and grabbed the 9mm from the glove compartment, sticking it behind his back. Fucking Jimmy. Had to play everything like a cowboy.

Soon as Deke stepped outside, the marijuana, earthy and pungent, penetrated his nasal membrane, burrowing deep in his throat. This shit with Kyle had him so on edge, he could use a bowl right now. Deke scoped out the woods, the hairs on his arm tingling with an electrical surge. More than Kyle that had him on edge.

Jimmy knocked on the front door, then jiggled the knob. No response. Nothing stirring. He pounded with the ball of his fist, then craned over his shoulder, nodding at the grubby kids playing in the dirt. "Someone's got to be here with all these little shits running around." He lit another cigarette. "Go check the other trailers, maybe he's back there."

"When's he ever back there?" Deke said. "Try the cell."

"No reception up here."

Deke reached for Jimmy's phone, twiddling his fingers until Jimmy slapped it in his palm. Deke stared at the screen. "One bar."

Jimmy snatched his phone back, punching in digits, glaring at Deke.

A ring tone sounded from inside the trailer.

The two men stared at each other, before slowly creeping around the side. Deke wiped dirt from the window, cupped his hands, and peered inside.

"Oh, fuck."

Deke started toward the front door.

"It's locked, man."

Deke turned around and ran to the back.

"What the fuck you doing? We need to get out of here."

Deke pointed at the barefoot kids squealing in the tall reeds. "And what? Leave them here?"

"What's getting inside going to do? They're all dead, man."

Deke shook him off and tugged at the handle, rattling the door, kicking the base and wrenching the metal frame. Jimmy came up beside him and grabbed his arm.

"How do you know someone ain't still in there?" Jimmy whispered.

Deke paused, contemplating the possibility.

"You worried about those kids?" Jimmy said. "We get up the road and call social services, place an anonymous call to the cops, whatever. But we need to leave. Now."

Deke nodded and Jimmy let him go, then Deke lifted his boot high and kicked in the door, the scent of fresh death smacking him in the face.

The blood around their heads appeared almost brown in the limited light, shimmering off the wood paneling like a new coat of shellac. Discharged casings lay scattered about. Three bodies. Deke counted four shells.

Jimmy followed him inside, gun in hand. "Holy shit."

Deke raised a finger to his lips, gestured for Jimmy to check the rest of the trailer. He dropped to a knee in front of Bodhi, whose face was frozen in death knell, eyes glassed over, mouth agape like he'd been in the middle of saying something.

"No one's here," Jimmy said. "But I found this." He held up a handgun, tucking his own away. "On the bed, like someone went to take a piss and forgot about it."

"We need to call the cops."

"And tell them what? We were up here visiting our drug dealer in the middle of the woods? I got a record, man. Cops ain't gonna believe shit we say."

"They're not gonna think we shot them. Why would we?"

Jimmy stared, deadpan. "Why wouldn't we?"

Deke pinched his eyes, unable to ignore the truth. Guys like Deke and Jimmy fit the profile. Enough for the cops to make their lives hell.

"Okay," Deke said. "We lock up and when we get to the Log Cabin, we'll make an anonymous call."

"Now you're thinking."

Someone pounded on the front door and rattled the knob. Jimmy reached for his piece, but Deke shook him off. He crept to the window and cracked the blinds. A dirty towheaded girl tried the handle again, before running off, distracted by whatever game her brothers and sisters were playing.

"Close that," Deke said, pointing at the back door he'd kicked in.

"You busted the lock."

"Check the bedroom, see if you can find something to tie it shut, rope, twine."

Deke stared down at his hands, which were stained with red splotches. He washed the blood off in the sink. He grabbed a chair from the table and jammed it under the broken handle, wiggling the seat to see if it would hold.

"Deke! Get in here!"

Deke darted into the next room where Jimmy stood motionless.

On the other side of the bed, two large canvas bags lay open, each stuffed with shrink-wrapped marijuana. Had to be a hundred pounds there.

"How'd you miss this the first time?"

"I was looking for someone who might want to shoot me.

Not fucking duffel bags stuffed with dope."

Deke scanned the tiny room, which was pointless. No closets to hide in, no chest of drawers to sneak behind. He started to drop down to check under the bed but Jimmy caught him by the shirt.

"Wood base. Solid."

"Why would someone leave it here?"

"Fuck if I know." Jimmy bent down and scooped a strap over his shoulder. "Grab the other one."

"Are you nuts? This shit belongs to someone."

"Yeah, Bodhi. And he ain't gonna need it. You know what we can sell this for?"

"Guys like me and you don't walk into free money."

"We did today." Jimmy readjusted the strap on his shoulder.

Deke didn't budge, but his stare lingered on the bag.

"Listen, ain't nobody know we been here. Just a bunch of snot-nosed kids who don't know who the hell we are. I'm sure Bodhi gets guys like us walking in and out all day long. Nobody gonna miss it."

"Of course somebody's gonna miss it!" Deke pointed to the other room. "You think they tied themselves up? Someone pulled the trigger."

"Yeah? Who? Where are they? We've been standing here, arguing next to a fucking window for the last ten minutes. Don't you think if someone was still here, we'd be dead by now?" Jimmy nodded toward the artillery shed. "Fucker's got enough guns in there to start a world war."

Deke looked past Jimmy and out the window, into the cool fog drifting down the mountain like dry ice. Anyone could be hiding in those woods.

Deke exhaled resignation, and hoisted the other bag.

In the kitchen, Jimmy rifled the dead man's pockets, pulling his cell phone, which he crushed with the heel of his boot.

"They'll get his phone records," Deke said.

"Like I don't use a burner." At the back door, he kicked aside the feeble chair Deke had set up, making for the artillery shed.

"They could've cleaned out the gun supply."

Jimmy rattled the keys. "Why would they clean out the guns and leave the pot? Doesn't make any sense."

"None of this does."

Jimmy headed up the hill to the gun shack.

"How we gonna lock up?" Deke shouted.

"We ain't."

Deke peered round the trailer, at the kids flying planes through twinberry sedge, getting chased by invisible monsters. The day was growing colder, and soon they'd want inside. He couldn't let them see this. He pulled his little Swiss army knife, the only gift the old man ever gave him, then headed in and sliced the twine off Bodhi's hands. Deke pulled the back door closed from the outside, threading twine through the handle hole several times, affixing the other end to the wrenched-out metal frame. He shook it. It'd do. At least against four- and five-year-olds.

When Jimmy returned, he had a gunnysack slung over his shoulder, tossing a box of shells in the air like an apple he'd plucked fresh from the tree.

"What's in the bag?" Deke asked, even though the answer was obvious.

Jimmy ignored the question and picked up the canvas bag. "There's another dead guy in the ammo trailer. Mexican."

"What are we gonna do?"

"Leave."

The children continued to race and squeal. The fog rolled in heavier. Dope and guns in tow, Deke and Jimmy hurried back to the truck. The lone thought racing through Deke's mind the entire time: this is a bad idea.

CHAPTER THREE

Lizzie didn't want to go the club tonight. It wasn't the hassle of sneaking in underage. Didn't matter if you were twenty or twelve; if you looked hot enough, the door guy at Liquid was letting you in. She was sick of the whole scene, the hours wasted getting ready, the pre-party ritual, slinking into tight skirts and tighter tops, listening to Melanie run down the flaws of all their friends, Lizzie knowing damn well if she wasn't there, Mel would be saying the same things about her. Then piling into some sweat box to be assaulted by excruciating, tub-thumping house music, waiting for this guy or that to come over and talk to you, so you could play a part, pretend to be something you're not, captivated by whatever hilarious thing he was saying, even though you couldn't hear a word, staring past his shoulder until his mouth stopped moving. Maybe it was being a child of hippies but Lizzie never liked the same music as her friends. She'd take Death Cab or Stars over whatever brainless hipster beat they were trotting out this week.

Then it was free drinks and whatever else anyone was handing out, because when you're a pretty girl you never have to pay for anything, all you have to do is decide what you are willing to give up to get it, and sometimes Lizzie didn't decide as much as she just let it happen, because she was too disinterested to stop it.

There was no pressing need right now. It was eight o'clock, plenty of time to figure out her Friday night.

Which was a lie. Lizzie knew once she sat down at her computer, Melanie would start DM'ing, and if she ignored those messages, the texts would start, followed by phone calls, and even if she turned off her cell, Melanie would ring her parents' landline, trying to convince them to make her go out. And the worst part? They would.

Lizzie decided she was staying in. Screw it. People can't make you do something you don't want to do. She threw on her Cal sweatshirt and went downstairs to curl up on the big couch with a bigger bowl of popcorn, find some mindless romantic comedy where everyone learns a lesson and goes home happy.

"Hey, kiddo," her father said when she rounded the corner into the kitchen. "What do you have planned for tonight?" He was sitting on a stool at the counter, drinking his single malt scotch like he did every evening after dinner, watching financial news on the laptop open next to him. They had more computers in their house than they did people.

"Think I'll hang out here."

"On a Friday night?" He peered up with an arched brow. "No dancing? Or maybe you're waiting for your dad to show you some fly moves?" Her dad mimed an exaggerated overbite, stiffly wriggling his shoulders.

Lizzie couldn't help but giggle. She often wondered what her father would've been like without her mom. In their moments alone, he was fun to be around. At least he'd retained a shred of authenticity.

Her mother emerged from the downstairs bathroom, face painted bright green, and her dad began humming the Wicked Witch of the East theme, his running joke whenever she wore the mint julep masque.

"Very funny, Dave. You should be thanking me for making the effort to stay beautiful for you."

Elizabeth Decker's whole life was a pursuit to thwart the ravages of time, and even Lizzie had to admit her mother looked remarkable for fifty-one. But it was not without serious investment. Spas and mud baths, daily trips to the health club, yoga and Pilates, not to mention the disgusting stuff that made Lizzie squirm, like coffee enemas and master cleanses, the details of which her mother would drop into casual conversation as though talking about switching detergent or trying a new olive oil.

"Did I hear you say you were staying in?" her mother asked.

"I'm tired. Plus I have a lot of studying."

"You've got the whole weekend to study."

"I think the last B you got was in the second grade," her father said, monitoring the intersecting, jagged graphs on his computer. "And if I recall, it was a B-plus. I'm sure you'll survive."

"Listen to your father. You should go out. If you don't want to drive, I'll be happy to drop you off and pick you up." Her mother's green face cracked with the forced smile.

"I can't believe your parents let you drink."

"What?"

Melanie slid over, repeating what she said by shouting it into Lizzie's ear.

"They don't let me drink."

"What?"

They'd been doing this same song and dance for the last hour, repeating every question and answer seventeen times. Lizzie grabbed her purse and yanked Melanie, who dragged her feet, across the dance floor. Scoring a booth at Liquid made you royalty. No one gave it up without a fight.

Lizzie struggled against the tide wading in, the sea of wasted bodies writhing against one another, strangers dry humping beneath pulsing lights, wrists and necks tethered with glowing neon bracelets. At the door, the jacked guy checking IDs unhooked the velvet rope that led outside to the smoking section.

Melanie rubbed her naked arms, stretching the hem of her short silver skirt, making a show of tapping her toes.

It *was* cold down by the water. But Melanie was also being

melodramatic. Both girls had spent their entire lives in San Francisco, no strangers to the drastic shifts in temperature. In SF, you go neighborhood to neighborhood. Where they were now, the piers, the frigid nighttime gusts off the Pacific whipped relentless.

Lizzie ignored her best friend's theatrics. Melanie pulled her phone and began texting. Lizzie gazed toward the docks, at the little schooners and big yachts. The bright Bay Bridge lights bounced off black water, city hills behind them twinkling like stars in the sky.

Whenever magazines boasted the Best Cities in America, San Francisco always hovered near the top, and you couldn't deny its many charms. But Lizzie was sick of hearing about them. San Francisco had its share of problems too. Like the homeless epidemic and soaring rents. The hipsters and irreverent douchebags who thought everything had to be ironic. Drove Lizzie nuts. You couldn't admit liking popular music or a movie like *Twilight*. Not that Lizzie harbored any love for the mainstream, and she deplored *Twilight*. But if someone *wanted* to like those things, what was the big deal? She detested the elitist mentality of the city, its cooler-than-cool vibe where earnestness painted a bullseye on your chest. Lizzie ached for something new.

"Why did you drag me out here?" Melanie said, stowing her cell back in her tiny square purse that mirrored a Japanese lunchbox. "You're not even smoking."

"Because I am tired of repeating myself twenty times."

"I'm freezing my ass off!" Melanie let out a sigh and dug back in her purse for the cigarettes she only smoked at clubs.

"My parents don't let me drink."

"Huh?"

"You said you couldn't believe my parents let me drink. But they don't."

"Then why are they always offering to pick you up at one in the morning? So you can have an extra Diet Coke?"

"They don't like me driving."

"Why? They bought you a goddamn Lexus. It's not like you'd have to borrow their car."

"They don't let me drink, okay?"

"Fine. They don't let you drink." Melanie took a drag and started scanning the crowded street.

Melanie wasn't right. But she wasn't far off. It's not like Lizzie's parents explicitly told her she could drink or were encouraging her to be an alcoholic. More like they granted a wide berth and didn't pry.

It was a stupid thing to get mad about, having parents who trusted you blithely, but Lizzie wouldn't mind a little brush back once in a while. You can't do anything right when nothing you do is wrong.

"I don't know why you're getting all worked up," Melanie said. "I wish I had your mom and dad."

"They're not so perfect."

"Whose parents are? They're better than most. Your mom actually wants to hear about your life."

"She just wants to be sure I use protection."

Both girls laughed.

Every time Melanie was over Lizzie's house, Elizabeth Decker would steer the conversation toward contraceptives, a not-so-subtle insinuation she knew the girls were sexually active and needed to be careful. Lizzie's mother could turn any current event into a PSA about condoms.

"Let's go somewhere else," Lizzie said.

"Like where?"

"I don't know. The Castro, get something to eat, walk around. Call Brenda and Jax, see what they're up to. Hang out somewhere different for a change. Maybe a coffee shop."

Melanie tugged the glittering fabric of her miniskirt. "You want to hang out at a coffee shop dressed like this?"

"It's the Castro, why not? Half the people there don't wear pants."

"Stop being so mopey," Melanie whined, pulling on her arm.

"You've been sulking all night. Let's have *fun*." She flicked her cigarette into the street even though there was an ashcan two feet away. "Come on. I know what will make you feel better."

They hadn't stepped two feet back in the club when Melanie pointed at the dreadlocked, wiry guy in the Charlie Brown sweater, chatting up the coat check girl.

It was easy to guess whom Melanie had been texting. The night growing late, she'd want something to make the party last, and that's what Tom—Lizzie's ex—was good for. That and computers.

"Hey, Lizzie," Tom said, strutting over with his lazy, affected gait. A lot of things about Tom drove Lizzie nuts, not the least of which was his white boy dreads. She had no problem with dreads. But one day Tom didn't have them, and the next he did. Lizzie wasn't sure how someone got dreadlocks, but she knew they didn't grow overnight.

"I thought you said you were going to Tahoe this weekend?" Lizzie said.

"Nah. My dad has some big case on Monday."

This was one of the reasons she stopped going with Tom. He was a goddamn liar. And he'd lie about weird, inconsequential shit. Like this Tahoe trip he told her about last weekend. Tom's father really was a lawyer, but there could've been a dozen reasons why they weren't making the trip, like his dad forgot to rent the gear or he'd gotten the weekend wrong, but the real reason probably didn't have anything to do with a case. Tom always felt the need to embellish, change minor details, make shit up.

"You have…anything?" Melanie whispered, which was pointless. With the music so loud, no one could hear what they were saying, and it's not like anyone would care if they could. Everybody at Liquid was on something.

"How 'bout you, Lizzie?" Tom asked. "You want to party?"

* * *

There are only so many lies you can tell yourself. Like threatening to stay home on a Friday night or pretending you're going to cool it with the pills for a while, even though you know you're not cooling anything. Not when it feels this good. Not when there is no problem, except the one you create in your own mind. This dance was part of the routine, the ritual, the habit. Like stopping at Happy Beans for cappuccinos before school, or watching *Gossip Girl* on Monday nights. It's what they did. They never had to talk about it, never had to make concrete plans. Yet every weekend seemed to play out the same. They'd run into someone on the scene, and next thing Lizzie knew they'd all be in a bathroom stall, drunk, giggling, dipping pinky fingers, placing pills under their tongues. The lights would go from staid to spectacular, and what was boring you senseless an hour ago, now you couldn't imagine living without, because dancing is fun, and this guy is fun, whatever his name is, your whole body buzzing, vision crystal blue, every cell inside you tingling, alive. You are awake and you are relevant, because it won't be until tomorrow that you start hating yourself again. At two a.m., you're just another club kid, watching the tracer lights, tasting tendrils of your own sweat-soaked hair and the cherry balm sticky on his lips. And tomorrow? Tomorrow is a long way off in the middle of the night.

CHAPTER FOUR

Kyle lay on the bed watching TV at the Skunk Train Inn. It was cool having more than six channels for a change. They even carried HBO and Cinemax, which Kyle knew showed plenty of skin from late nights at Ronnie's. He flipped through the guide to see if any of his father's movies were coming on, but after scanning ahead several hours, he stopped checking. Kyle didn't get the impression they'd be there long.

Deke hadn't said much since he had Kyle pack up, the two of them fleeing into the night like a pair of refugees. Kyle didn't have a lot to bring along. A tattered photo of his mom and dad together, the only one he had of either, faded, yellowed, curled at the edges. Some poems Kyle had written that he never showed anyone. The letters that his father had stopped sending years ago. All stuffed in an old shaving bag. Pretty sad when he thought about it like that. An entire lifetime fit in a shoebox.

Kyle glanced at the clock. Eleven-thirty-three p.m. They'd been at the motel for three hours, his cousin bolted to the same spot by the window. The only time he moved was when he went outside to smoke and make a phone call he didn't want Kyle hearing. Whenever Kyle asked a question, his cousin told him to shut up, so Kyle stopped asking questions.

The Skunk Train, like most of the roadsides on the Highway, functioned primarily as a hole-up for transients and derelicts, or a pit stop for tourists on their way to Eureka; it was no place you wanted to call home. Deke's trailer was no prize but it beat this place. Pulling in the lot, Kyle had spied several withered men sitting on folding patio chairs outside front doors, stubbled and unkempt, staring with dead eyes at passing cars as they drank beer from plastic cups.

Since Kyle started hanging out on the Highway, he'd see these guys carrying plastic grocery bags from Geiger's, or riding rickety bicycles back to their motel rooms, and he couldn't help wondering how they ended up here. Depressed the hell out of him thinking about it. No one is born in a place like the Skunk Train. Who'd sign up for that ride? Sometimes Kyle worried he'd already punched his ticket, and the real question wasn't if he was already onboard, but how far down the line it would take him.

Kyle reached for the phone on the nightstand.

"What the fuck you doing?"

"Calling Ronnie."

"No, you're not."

Kyle let go the receiver and pushed himself up on the bed. "How long do we have to stay here?"

"You bitch about not having cable at the house. You got cable. Watch it."

"Nothing's on." Kyle switched off the TV. "Can I at least have a cigarette?"

Deke looked at him like he had six heads.

"What? You said you knew I smoked."

"Yeah, said I knew. Not liked. Big fucking difference."

There was a light rap on the door. Deke motioned for Kyle to be quiet and gripped the 9mm in his waistband, peeking around the curtain. He let go the gun and unlatched the chain, letting in Jimmy, who was toting a gunnysack.

Deke shut the door behind him and refastened the locks.

"What the fuck took you so long?"

"How easy you think it is unloading a hundred pounds of pot in the middle of the night?

"Keep your voice down," Deke said, nodding toward Kyle.

Jimmy dropped the gunnysack overflowing with firearms beside the two canvas bags stuffed with dope. "You think he's a fucking idiot? He knows what's going on." Jimmy turned to Kyle. "Yo, Kyle. You a fucking idiot?"

"Screw you, Jimmy."

"See," Jimmy said. "Bright boy."

Deke reached for his cigarettes. He crumpled the empty pack. "Give me a smoke."

"Me too," Kyle said.

Jimmy looked at Deke with mocked surprise.

Deke waved his hand. "Give him a fucking cigarette. He's been stealing mine for years."

Jimmy sat down at the small, round table, slid out two cigarettes, and tossed the pack and matches to Kyle. "So here's the deal—"

Deke stopped him. He took out his wallet, extracting a twenty. "Kyle, go grab us something to eat."

"Like what?"

"I don't care. Get a pizza or something."

"I'm not hungry."

"I didn't ask if you were hungry."

"Why can't I stay here?"

"Don't give me a hard time, okay? Please."

Kyle couldn't remember Deke ever saying please. Something about the way he said it, too, like he couldn't take one more bit of bad news, made Kyle pop up and snatch the bill from his hand.

Deke opened the door and leaned next to his ear. "Don't take too long. Pick up a pizza, chow mein, whatever, and come right back. You understand?"

"Yeah, Deke. I understand. I'm not a moron." He looked back at Jimmy and held up the lit cigarette. "Thanks for the smoke."

* * *

25

Kyle wished he'd put on a jacket before he left. The cold, salty fog invaded Spy Rock and the Ranges, dimming streetlights and making his teeth chatter. The Highway didn't get much traffic this time of night, mainly motorcycles making for the Ironside, or tractor trailers shortcutting the mountains to avoid the interstate. When the big machines would blow past, they'd whip up dirt and stone, blasting his skin raw.

There was a Chinese restaurant across the divide, handpainted signs advertising cheap Kung Po combos with free egg roll, but Kyle wouldn't eat at Kowloon's if you paid him. Not long ago the restaurant got caught using cat meat.

Why should he have to walk in the freezing cold so Deke and Jimmy could argue over nickels and dimes? It wasn't that complicated. You want to sell pot, you go to the Ironside. Plus, the biker bar had burgers.

The Ironside was a mile or so up the road, which in this weather seemed a lot farther. Being underage, Kyle never went inside the bar. The Ironside had an outdoor patio, bikers kicking it there or in the parking lot. Tonight's crowd seemed more raucous than usual. He could hear the party from up the street.

Soon as Kyle stepped around back he began wondering if this was a good idea. Harleys rumbled past. Headlights fanned over the disturbed gravel and dust, spreading up the old wood walls. Some of the boards were rotted straight through. Hardfaced women squealed on the back steps every time a guy slapped them on the butt.

He was about to hightail it when someone called out.

"Little brother!"

Kyle recognized Eason, an old-school biker with a Santa Claus beard and potbelly. Kyle had sold to him before. He was nice, like a cool grandpa. He always called Kyle "little brother." Eason sat straddling his hog, smoking a cigarette and drinking beer beneath the porch light by the big blue dumpsters. When Kyle got closer, another man he didn't recognize stepped out of the shadows, zipping his fly. Gangly with black, pitted eyes, the stranger had pale yellow skin the color of a gas station egg yolk.

Eason swatted the man on the shoulder. "Sonny, this's my pal...Carl."

"Kyle."

"Right. Kyle. Where's your bike, little brother?" Eason and Sonny traded smirks, like it was a private joke Kyle wasn't getting. "What you doing out so late?"

"I was hungry."

"You want me to send Sonny in get you a burger? They got some tasty burgers."

Kyle fished out the twenty-dollar bill. "I need three."

"Three, it is." Eason gestured for Sonny to take the money.

The gaunt man plucked the bill from his hand and disappeared inside.

"So that the *only* reason you came down here? Or maybe you got something you need to unload? 'Cause you got something, I'm buying." Eason laughed, but not like he thought anything was funny. "You got good timing, little brother. Place's been drier'n shit. Weird, like nobody got nothin'."

Kyle shook his head. The way Eason was leering at him now, like a hungry bobcat licking its chops, Kyle regretted coming down here so late. He normally dropped by during the day, when it was a bunch of dudes joking on motorcycles, drinking beers and hanging out. The nighttime was different. Eason seemed whiskey mean.

"Sure you don't," Eason said to himself, pulling a half pint from his leather vest and taking a long, hard pull.

Eason offered his bottle. "You're looking jumpy there, little brother. Need a swig?" Before Kyle could respond, Eason jerked it back. "What am I thinking? Offering alcohol to a minor? I don't want to get in trouble with the law. You ain't workin' with the fuzz, are you, Kyle?" Eason cackled. In the porch light shining down, Kyle could see his decayed teeth, browned and blackened nubs rotted to the root. He didn't remind Kyle of Santa Claus anymore.

"I should get going. My cousin's waiting for me."

"What about your burgers?"

"That's okay. You and your friend can have them."

"Hey, kid. You sure you or maybe…your cousin…don't have something? Make it worth your while."

Sonny came out the back door with the greasy, brown sack, jamming the bag hard into Kyle's sternum.

"Where you staying?" Eason asked Kyle. "You need a ride? Hop on. I'll give you a ride back. It's cold. You don't got a jacket. You'll freeze, little brother. I got an extra helmet."

"No. Thank you. My cousin's waiting. In his truck. Him and some friends. A lot of friends. I gotta go."

Kyle beelined for the road as more motorcycles roared past. He walked fast as he could without making it appear he was running away. He could feel their eyes boring into the back of his head. When he got around the corner, he leaned against the building, crouching to catch his breath. He didn't know why his heart was beating so fast.

Then he took off sprinting up the Highway.

CHAPTER FIVE

"I already explained what happened," Craven said.

"Explain it again." Doyle fit the clip, racking the slide. The action made a loud, startling click.

The other man, McKay, sat on the couch. Two girls in the kitchen, neither of whom could've been older than eighteen, stopped what they were doing to watch.

Craven gazed out the window into the dark night, the sky above the lakeside cabin full of stars. It was sure peaceful out here.

Doyle clanked the butt of the gun off the table. This had always been Craven's problem. If he weren't so easily distracted, he wouldn't be in this mess.

"What was I supposed to do?"

"See if Bodhi's holding. Then I send someone a fucklot smarter than you to take care of it." Doyle stood up and tucked the gun behind his pants. A burly, barrel-chested bear of a man who'd spent his whole life in these Humboldt woods, Lester Doyle knew how to intimidate.

"Someone drove up the driveway," Craven said. "Thought it was the cops."

"You thought one cop car was gonna, what? Pop in, ask some questions?"

"I already explained—"

"Explain it again!" Doyle slammed his fist down on the table. The girls gasped, before the air was sucked from the room.

"Explain to me again how you left over a hundred pounds of dope behind."

Craven squirmed, haunches up like a misbehaving brat expecting a head cuff.

"Tell me again how a dumb fuck like you shoots three people—"

"Four," drawled McKay, peering over the cushions. "Don't forget the Mexican." He rolled up and grabbed a poker, stoking the flames to keep the cabin toasty warm.

"Right. Wouldn't want to forget the Mexican." Doyle sneered. "*Four* people dead, one of them a member of the goddamn cartel. You think they're gonna, what? Forget about that? Have their accountants write it off on this year's fucking taxes?"

Craven showed his hands, making it clear he had no fight in him. Him and Doyle went way back. Craven had one play. Tell the truth, throw himself at the boss's mercy, get the chance to make it up to him later.

But Doyle's eyes didn't betray a man willing to give anyone a break tonight.

"Things got out of hand, man," Craven whined. "You got those fucking rug-rats running around outside, you can't even think, it's so loud, and you know how Bodhi is, paranoid conspiracy mutherfucker, going off about microchips and fluoride in the drinking water. And then the Mexican shows up. He's at the door with two big bags of the shit. Ding dong. A regular door-to-door salesman. Then everyone's staring at me, all accusatory—"

"Sure," McKay said from the couch. "Bodhi's the paranoid one."

"The Mexican starts eyeballing me, asking Bodhi what my story is, what I'm doing there, and then *Bodhi* starts getting suspicious. Those two bitches won't stop squawking. I want to jet but I can't. The Mexican made a move. I thought it best if I made it look like an execution, y'know? For when the cops find 'em. Drug deal gone bad."

"Sounds like someone got too high on his own product,"

McKay sing-songed.

"Those weren't cops!"

"I know that. Now. But at the time...they're gonna find 'em eventually, right? I didn't want anything traced back to us."

Doyle stuck a finger in Craven's face. "How the hell's it an execution, Einstein, when the guy you allege did the shooting is locked in the ammo shed, with a bullet in his brain?"

"Maybe it was a shootout or something?" The explanation had sounded a lot better in Craven's head when he was running through it earlier. But earlier he'd smoked more, had chilled himself out. Now he was riled, worried, twitchy, which can make someone look guilty even when they're not.

"Then the dead man what? Gets up, walks, and locks himself in the shed?"

"I wasn't thinking—"

"No. You weren't."

"What did you do with your gun?" McKay asked. "That's right, you got some weird kink for pissing outdoors."

"It's not a sex thing. I find it...liberating."

"Next time you want to be liberated," McKay said, "might want to check to make sure the door's unlocked, so you can get back inside. Y'know, for when the cops who turn out not to be cops show up."

"Fuck you, McKay. I don't have to explain shit to you."

"But you do to me." Doyle pulled his gun and planted it square between Craven's eyes.

Maybe friendship didn't matter as much as Craven thought.

"I can get it back! I know how to get it back!"

Doyle studied him a moment, then lowered his firearm. "Keep talking."

"That's what I've been trying to tell you," Craven said, speeding along the plan he'd just begun formulating. "I know one of the guys. In the truck that showed up."

"You know him?"

"Not know-know, but, yeah, I know who he is. Jimmy

something something. McDermott! Jimmy McDermott. Lives down in Dormundt. Works at a tattoo parlor on the Highway. Bones and something. Small time. Got a partner."

"Who?"

"I don't know his name. But I've seen them both up at Bodhi's before."

"Volume?"

"Nah, man, I'm tellin' ya, small time. A pound at most."

"You sure it was him?"

"Positive. I saw him and his buddy drag the bags off and load them in the truck."

"When you was hiding in the woods like a bitch."

"Fuck you, McKay."

Doyle hoisted a hand for everyone to shut up. Craven could see Doyle mulling it over in his brain. As long as Doyle saw a way out of this, better yet the possibility of turning a colossal fuck-up into a profit, Craven would get a second chance.

Doyle glanced at McKay. "What do you think?"

McKay grumbled and groaned but consented. "Could pin the Mexican on this Jimmy guy. We get the shit back in time."

"That's what I'm saying," said Craven, perking up.

"Shut up." Doyle ran a meaty palm over his bristles. "Okay. We got to move fast. Soon as the Mexicans get wind of this, they're gonna to be out for blood. And I'm guessing numbnuts here—" Doyle and McKay both flashed on Craven, "—left something behind that could send them our way."

"I didn't leave any—"

Doyle pointed a finger at his face. "Not another fucking word."

The two girls were huddled by the kitchen window, staring out into the night.

"Yo, ladies. What's so fascinating out there?"

The girls didn't answer right away.

"Hey!" Doyle snapped. "I said what is it?"

One of the girls, a petit blonde in teeny cutoff shorts and a

Rancid tank top, turned over her shoulder. "There's a car outside."

"Doing what?"

"Nothing. Just sitting there with its lights off."

CHAPTER SIX

Kyle kept checking over his shoulder. He hadn't been able to make his legs slow down no matter how hard he tried. All the way back to the motel, where now he stalked around in the parking lot, seething. He hated how scared he'd get over the dumbest things. He felt nauseated. He wanted to blame it on the greasy stench from the burger bag but knew that wasn't it. He'd acted like coward, a little baby running from the big bad bikers. It was that goddamn Sonny's fault. Dude looked like a cadaver, hollow and waxen.

No, this was on Deke for dragging him down here so he and Jimmy could pretend they were in the movies. That was the problem with Dormundt. Nothing but small-time hustlers trying to act like big shots.

This town was the reason his life sucked, why he couldn't get a girlfriend and fought with everyone, why his grades were failing and he hated everything. The world had to be bigger than two donut shops and a bank, and if someone didn't see that, didn't make a move to take their shot, he deserved whatever fate he got.

From outside the room, Kyle could hear Deke and Jimmy arguing again. It sounded like they were one insult away from throwing down. Once Kyle knocked, they shut up, even if no one rushed to answer the door.

"Come on! It's freezing balls out here. Let me in."

The door swung inward and Kyle shoved the bag of burgers

into his cousin's gut.

"You're welcome."

Kyle mean mugged Deke, but his cousin was too busy glowering at Jimmy, who sat at the table sucking on a cigarette, his sinewy, tattooed arm slung over the back of the chair.

"Go on," Deke said. "Keep talking. Kyle's family. No reason to keep anything from him. Affects him the same."

Jimmy scoffed.

Kyle sat on the bed.

Deke tossed the burgers into a chair and looked over. "What took so long?"

"I went to the Ironside to get burgers."

"What the hell you go down there for? I said get pizza. Christ, there's a Chinese place across the street. Why can't you do anything I ask?"

"I wanted a burger. And you didn't tell me *where* to go, so that's where I went."

Jimmy reached across the table into the sack and snatched a burger. He turned to Kyle. "Where's the ketchup?"

"Didn't have any."

"What do you mean didn't have any? Who the fuck eats a burger without ketchup?"

"He said they didn't have any. Who gives a shit? We have bigger problems than you not having fucking ketchup for your hamburger." Deke gestured at the two big bags on the floor. "Someone is going to be looking for that."

"I told you," Jimmy said, standing up and rifling the sack like he had a better chance of finding ketchup if he was on two feet, "I have a buyer right now. But the price is the price. You can't have it both ways, Deke. You want to unload fast, we're gonna take a hit."

"Twenty-five cents on the dollar isn't a hit. It's fucking rape."

Jimmy shrugged.

"How far you think you'll get with fifty thousand? 'Cause we sure as shit can't stay in Dormundt after this."

"I don't know where *you're* going, man. But I have plenty of options. That money is my ticket out of this dump."

"We can go see my dad," Kyle said.

"Will you shut up about your father? Don't you think if he wanted anything to do with you, he would've called by now? Jesus, Kyle. Give it a rest."

Kyle wanted to hurl back something hurtful, an insult that would gut good, but his throat choked up, and no words came out.

"Hey, man. I'm sorry. I didn't mean it. This shit has me all fucked up, all right?"

Kyle knew if he said anything he'd start crying, so he just nodded.

"You know what, man. Maybe that's not such a bad idea. SoCal. You up for a road trip? You want to go see your dad? Okay, we'll go see Dad." Deke turned to Jimmy. "Set it up."

Jimmy tore a hunk of beef, making a slow show of gnashing the pulpy wad, before swallowing it down in one exaggerated gulp. He dropped the sandwich, sucked the meaty bits through his teeth, wiped his hands down the front of his shirt, saluted, and left.

Deke dragged his fingers through his hair and went back to breathing hard through his nose.

"You mean it?"

Deke nodded but didn't turn around.

Kyle wanted to ask more questions, like if Deke even knew where to look. But he didn't want him to get mad and change his mind, so Kyle didn't say anything.

A few minutes later, Jimmy returned. "All good. He's gonna call from Kowloon's across the street. I'll scope it out, make sure everything is copacetic. Then we drive back here and you bring out the shit."

"How we know the guy's not a narc?"

"This ain't my first rodeo. Something seems off, I'll be able to tell. Chip Morsman deals with this dude all the time."

"The same Chip Morsman that Deke beat up?"

"Ancient history, bro." Jimmy winked at Kyle, before jetting out the door.

"Fucking asshole," Deke muttered.

"Are we really going to L.A.?"

"Jesus, I already said yes, didn't I?" Deke raked his hands over his eyes and sat on the edge of the bed next to Kyle. "Yes. We are. First we're going to have to find him."

"Can't be too hard."

"You know how big Los Angeles is?"

"I mean, because he's so famous. We can call the studios—"

"You can't call up Paramount and ask for a directory, Kyle." Deke struck a match and lit another smoke.

"Your dad must know where he is."

"Yeah, him. I don't know where he lives either." Deke waved out the burning match head.

"San Francisco, right? It's his brother." Kyle never met his uncle, and Deke never talked about him. "He has to be able to give us *something*."

Deke reached in his pocket and pulled out the Swiss army knife, passing it along.

"What's this?"

"Last thing the old man gave me. Hell, the only thing the prick gave me."

"Why don't you talk about him?"

"He's not worth talking about."

Kyle went to hand the pocketknife back.

"Keep it. Fucking thing hasn't done me any good."

Kyle tucked the pocketknife away. "If we can't find your dad, how will we find mine?"

"I don't know, man." Deke tossed his head back with a long groan. "You ask so many goddamn questions."

Kyle waited a moment.

"Hey, Deke?"

"Yeah."

"Why you hang out with Jimmy if he gives you such a pain in the ass?"

Deke laughed. "That's the smartest question you asked all night, little brother. Sometimes I do not know." He paused. "I guess because there aren't a whole lot of people I trust. Jimmy can be an asshole, but he's true blue. You can count on him to do the right thing when it matters."

"You ever been to L.A.?"

"Long time ago. Don't remember much. Sunshine, bright colors, beaches, girls in bikinis on roller skates, that kind of shit."

"You think I'll like it?"

"Probably not."

"Why not?"

"Because you don't like anything. You walk around moping all the time. Or you're fighting with everybody."

"I don't fight with everybody."

"You don't understand how this world works. You got your head in the clouds and stars in your eyes."

"You're crazy."

"You don't have any friends."

"I have Ronnie—"

"I've never seen you with a girlfriend. I know you *like* girls because you get into all my *Penthouses* and leave your crusty, stiff-ass tube socks everywhere."

"Girls don't go with guys like me."

"Who do they go with then?"

"Guys who play sports or have cars, guys who don't look like me."

"What's wrong with the way you look?"

Kyle scoffed.

"Hey, we're related. So if you say you're not good looking, then you're saying *I'm* not good looking. And everyone knows I'm the best looking guy in Dormundt."

"That's damning with faint praise." Even though Kyle knew

he was right. Girls in Dormundt did go crazy over Deke. More importantly, he carried himself like he knew it.

"You need to have more confidence. You have a lot going for you."

"Yeah, my dad's a big shot in Hollywood. My dad who won't talk to me."

"Fuck him. I'm talking about *you*."

"What about me?"

"We already covered how good looking you are." Deke smirked.

Kyle didn't think it was funny the first time, and he wasn't laughing now. "What else?" When Deke didn't answer right away, Kyle said, "That's what I thought."

"How am I supposed to answer that? I don't know what I got going for *me*."

"Girls like you. You don't take shit from anybody. You're tough."

"Is that why you quit going to school? People were picking on you?"

"No one notices me. At least not the people I want to notice me. Certainly not girls. Down on the Highway, at least I'm the guy with the weed. But I don't want to end up there. I want to be something more."

"You have time. You're not even sixteen yet."

"Soon enough."

"Trust me. You're better off where you are, where you have a safety net."

"What safety net?"

"Me. What do you think? As long as I'm around, I won't let anything happen to you." He put a hand on Kyle's shoulder. "I know we fight a lot, but I love you, man."

With those words all resistance dropped. Though he didn't want to, Kyle couldn't stop the tears from falling. Deke didn't say anything else, just swung his arm around him and let him cry. Kyle cried for a good, long time.

CHAPTER SEVEN

The buzzing cell woke Deke.

"Go time," Jimmy said.

Deke rubbed his eyes and checked the clock on the bedside. A little after three. Kyle lay sound asleep. "What the hell took you so long?"

"Had to make sure everything's kosher."

"Thought you were meeting the guy across the street."

"I did. You want to do this or not?"

"It's three in the fucking morning. Don't you think it's going to look suspicious?"

"What? Walking outside? Jesus, stop being such a pussy."

Deke took a deep breath. Maybe he was overreacting. Everyone slung up here. If it weren't for pot deals, Dormundt's economy would dry up.

"Come outside in five minutes."

Deke hung up the phone and grabbed his cigarettes. He stared down at Kyle sleeping peacefully. Boy didn't even have peach fuzz yet. Deke both envied and pitied him. It'd be nice to have another crack. But there wasn't enough money in the world to make Deke go through his teens again.

There were so many things Deke wished he could've said to Kyle during their heart-to-heart, if that's what you'd call it. They hadn't had many moments like that, where Deke wasn't pissed and Kyle wasn't defensive, where they could communicate without it coming to blows. Deke had wanted to tell him everything, explain all the shit that had been too painful to talk about over the years, but he was lousy at expressing himself. He regretted the way he'd lose his temper and lash out. He wished he could take it back. No doubt the kid was screwed up. He could see the hurt in his eyes.

Deke had been on his own most of his life, which forced him to accept some cold, hard truths early on. Nobody owes you anything, and they give you even less. Like Kyle, he had no mom, same good-for-nothing father. Deke had worked damn hard to make a better life for himself. Had his own apartment at sixteen, owned a house by the time he was twenty. It wasn't much, but it was all his. Dealing, hustling, scrap metal, construction, bartending, whatever it took. They shared the same blood, but Kyle didn't have what Deke had inside him. Deke had done the best he could with a bad situation. He'd made so many mistakes. It was okay. There was still plenty of time to get it right.

Deke peeled back the curtains as car headlights appeared in the motel parking lot. He stubbed out his cigarette in the ashtray, untucked his shirt over his gun, and grabbed the two large bags by the side of the bed. Damn things felt like cinder block engines double-dipped in cement.

At the door, Deke paused to look back at Kyle. He thought about waking him to tell him to stay inside but decided to let him sleep. This would all be over in a few. Then they'd split the money, and he and Kyle would hit the 101 South, go find the big-shot movie man in Hollywood. It was about time.

The thick fog rolled in thicker, the cold night harboring a cruel winter bite. It hurt to breathe in. Passing the ice machine, its low thrum rattling his nerves, Deke spotted the car, a white four-door, parked with its lights off beside Jimmy's red truck in the smoky shadows. A familiar tattooed arm appeared in the unrolled window. Deke lugged the heavy bags till it felt like his shoulders were being wrenched from their sockets. He dropped them by the passenger side.

"This is my boy," Jimmy said to the driver.

Doubling over to catch his breath, Deke peered through the dim glow of dashboard lights. The man appeared to be in his forties, clean-shaven, strong chin. More leading man than drug dealer.

"Let's see what you boys got."

Jimmy raised his eyebrows.

Deke unzipped the bags, the man not offering more than a cursory glance.

"It's all there," Jimmy said.

The man popped the trunk.

"Aren't you forgetting something?"

The man hefted a backpack from between his feet and unzipped it. Stacks of banded hundred-dollar bills. "Satisfied?"

Jimmy nodded toward the back, and Deke lugged the bags once more, biceps on fire. He'd just hoisted the second bag in the trunk when he caught the swirling lights out the corner of his eye, fiery reds registering before he could appreciate what was happening.

There came the quick burst of a siren, followed by megaphone hiss. Then both cut out, leaving only high beams and dead country silence.

Deke threw up his forearm to block the blinding glare, squinting and twisting away from the spotlight, creeping back toward the front of the car, passenger side.

"*Weapons on the ground! Hands behind your head and get on your knees!*"

Inside the car, Jimmy palmed the dash. The driver had his badge out and gun trained, the money resting on the center console, so close and yet so far away. He winked at Deke, bright blue eyes glinting. Fucking undercover. What made Deke think he and Jimmy could pull off a deal this big?

The instructions came again, louder, clearer, losing patience: "*Get on the fucking ground and put your fucking hands behind your head! Or we shoot!*"

Deke had dropped his gun and was falling to his knees, when the loud throttle of motorcycles roared into the parking lot, augmented tailpipes coughing thunder. The bikes split up, wishboning right and left. Deke peered around the flatbed. A fat biker with a white beard had his sawed-off .30/06 leveled on the unmarked cop car. On the opposite side, a gaunt man who looked like walking death cocked his shotgun.

"Police!" an unsure voice called from out of the blackness. "Put the guns down and get—"

"Fuck you, pig! You put *your* guns down, mutherfucker. We got you—"

The first blast ripped through the icy Humboldt night. Then came the rapid fire of handguns, like a string of firecrackers on the Fourth.

Deke cradled his head and ducked down, as the driver kicked open his door and took cover behind it. Jimmy followed suit and hit the ground, writhing through the dirt on his belly, toward the woods behind the motel. Staggering to his feet, Jimmy fell into a run and disappeared into the forest.

At the open door, Deke jabbed a hand into the front seat and snared the backpack, flinging it over the rails into the flatbed of Jimmy's truck. Crouching, he swiveled and reached for the truck's handle. Locked. He felt the keys in his pocket. Wrong keys. Wrong truck. His was parked on the other side of the motel. With shotguns booming and bullets whizzing past, he couldn't think. Deke scoured the gravel for the gun he'd dropped, steeling resolve...

Kyle.

He had to get to Kyle. The fat biker blocked his direct path. His quickest route: an end around, trace the edge of the woods and follow the side of the road, sneak in from behind.

Gunfire crackling all around, Deke covered up, running toward the tree line. He heard someone scream and go down, but he couldn't see who was winning the firefight. He didn't care. He had to get back the motel room. Scenery blurred past, branches bending and snapping, stinging arms and legs with cracks of a whip.

Coming out of the woods along the Highway, Deke fought to right himself, stumbling until he hit full stride. The ground shaky beneath his feet, he craned his neck in time to catch the fat biker take a gut shot and drop, a final errant sawed-off blast echoing skyward.

Turning toward the hotel, he saw the boy in the window, face pressed to the glass. Their eyes locked a moment and everything stopped.

He came out of it when the tractor trailer blared its horn. Deke snapped his head around as sixty thousand pounds of steel barreled down on him.

Maybe there wouldn't be time after all.

CHAPTER EIGHT

Lizzie turned over into the lump beside her, then turned back and stared at the wall, which was plastered with frameless posters that screamed college dorm: Jack Johnson without shoes jamming on guitar; the famous one of the sailor molesting the nurse after WWII; and one of those cheesy, obligatory lists about why beer is better than women, stainless steel stein resting between an enormous pair of surgically enhanced breasts.

She remembered liking his sense of humor. He'd made her laugh when she wasn't in the mood to find anything funny, and that helped. Of course so did rolling hard on Molly, and by the time they hooked up, she was rolling pretty hard.

After Tom kicked down, he and Lizzie bickered the way exes do, which made her drink more, get nastier, planting subtle insults like a poison pill, until he split, and Melanie had zeroed in on the frat pack of douchebags, Melanie's usual M.O.

Lizzie had been rude to him at first. To his credit, he hadn't forced it, took the hint and laid off. After a while, she decided he was different than his buddies, so she'd given him a chance. And he *was* cute, with the sort of look Lizzie liked, shaggy hair and that skinny rocker body. Melanie teased her endlessly about her taste in boys.

But now she was having second thoughts. His room—she couldn't remember his name—Steve? Sean? Scott!—was a such a frat-boy cliché. PlayStation, requisite bong and white boy reggae art, empty cans of Pabst. She even spotted a puka shell necklace. More than one, in fact.

Lizzie slipped out of bed and slinked her top back over her head. Downstairs she could hear the housemates in the kitchen making breakfast. She didn't mind the walk of shame. One of the benefits of being raised by ex-hippies: a healthy view of sex. What irked her was how they'd shut up, avert eyes, grumble a bashful hello, like they were decent human beings and not immature pricks, and the second she was out the front door, they'd bust up laughing, whooping and high-fiving one another. Double standards drove her bat shit. These guys go out to hook up, and they think less of any girl they get. And the girls who don't give it up are teases. She'd grown so sick of this game.

A ride home was the least he could do.

After a couple ineffective coughs, she climbed back in bed to have a little fun first. She bounced up and down. Then jabbed her knuckle into his shoulder blade and twisted. He stirred, returning a sleepy smile, which quickly turned into scrambling up the bed with wide-eyed panic. Never failed to make her laugh. When they're drunk and horny, nobody cares. In the sober morning light, words like "statutory" become very real.

"Hi," Lizzie said, twirling a finger through her hair.

He pulled the bedspread over him and glanced around the room.

"You mind giving me a ride home? I don't have my license yet." Lizzie crawled on all fours toward him. "I'm not in any rush."

"Um, how...old are you?"

She grabbed the covers and tugged on them. "You didn't care last night." This was almost too easy.

"You were in an eighteen-and-over club."

"Right," Lizzie said, her hand inching down his chest, "because no one ever uses a fake ID."

Scott jumped out of bed, pulling the sheets with him. "Seriously, how old are you?"

"Fourteen," she said, nibbling her lip. "Well, almost like

fourteen and a half."

"Jesus Christ. Oh fuck. Oh fuck."

She slid back on her haunches. "Relax. I'm fucking with you. I'm seventeen. I'll be eighteen in a couple months. And don't worry. If you give me a ride home, I promise I won't call the cops."

The light splintered a brilliant kaleidoscope through the tall redwood trees onto the blood-splattered gravel. Workers set numbered placards by a pair of bodies before covering them with white sheets.

Cutting Detective Marc Jacobs sat in the abandoned white Nissan, hands gripping the wheel. He stared out the windshield toward the woods. It was standard operating procedure for Dormundt to outsource its major crimes to larger surrounding municipalities such as Cutting or Richter. Could've gone either way. Cutting got the call. Tough luck, Richter. He climbed out and started toward the Highway.

A long line of traffic backed up for miles as EMTs worked to scrape up body parts and pieces of brain. The perp had been struck by a tractor trailer doing sixty-five and gotten caught in the undercarriage and dragged beneath its wheels, blood streaking pavement for the hundred or so yards it had taken the driver to stop. A fifth wheel wrecker was hooked up to wrench the semi out of the culvert where it had jackknifed.

Detective Jacobs studied the placement of the bodies, the two bikes that lay like dead horses in the Wild West dust. He made his way to the center of the lot, crouching in the middle of ticker tape swath, examining the tracks. He began to construct a scenario. The Nissan came in first and was waiting. Then the second car, followed by the bikers. A gunfight ensued. The bikers lost. In the dirt at his feet, you could see where another truck had peeled out in a hurry. It added up. Only thing left to do was connect the dots.

One of Dormundt's finest approached. "Thanks for getting out here so fast, detective." The young cop shook his head. "What a bloodbath, eh?" He fished a half-eaten breakfast sandwich from his jacket pocket and started noshing.

"What's your take on this?" Detective Jacobs asked.

The officer unplugged the cheesy eggs from his pie hole, wadding the sandwich back into his pocket. He pointed down the Highway. "My guess? Drug deal gone sour."

"What makes you say that?"

"It's Dormundt." He faked a laugh.

"Take me through it. The gunshot victims?"

"Ironside. Biker bar down the road. Those guys are bad mutherfuckers. That fat dead one over there, one looks like Santa Claus? Name's Cord Eason, did twenty in San Quentin. Murder two." He pointed at the other body. "That's Sonny Castille. Remember the Oakdale Murders? He was—"

"I get it. They're badasses." Jacobs nodded at the white Nissan. "How about that?"

"Ran the plates. Reported stolen."

"You really pinning this on a bunch of hillbillies?"

"That's the weird thing." The officer lowered his voice. "Talked to some guests at the motel. Said before the bikers showed up...cops were here."

"Cops?"

"At least they *identified* themselves as cops. Saw the lights. Heard them shout it, loud and proud."

"One of your boys?"

"Naw, not a regular squad car. You know how small Dormundt is. Unmarked. A dashboard light." He panned left, right, whispered, "Want to know what I think?"

"That's why I asked," Jacobs replied with a good-natured smile.

"You can order one of those dashboard lights on the internet. Pick up a phony badge too."

"Someone impersonating a police officer?"

"You get a lot of cowboys up here. About three years ago a guy pulled the same stunt. Although that was to get a woman to flash her, well, boobs."

"Interesting theory, officer. Where's the drugs? The money?"

The eager beaver had no response.

Jacobs nodded at the EMTs stuffing what was left of the one man into a giant black trash bag. "We're supposed to believe a guy dumb enough to run into a semi took out two badass bikers with shotguns? Scared off couple more playing dress up?"

"Lucky shot?"

"Wasn't any lucky shot." Jacobs pointed at two sets of foot-prints, one wrapping end around, up to the Highway where the man was run over, the other leading into the woods.

"Two sets of prints."

"More than one man." Jacobs paused long enough to let that sink in. When the officer didn't come around quick enough, Jacobs stoked the flame. "These were pros."

"A heist?"

Jacobs shrugged, answering without answering.

The officer scratched his chin, face screwed up, half buying in, half still confused. "Yeah, I guess that makes more sense."

"Don't worry," Jacobs said. "You'll get it. You do this as long as I have, this stuff becomes second nature."

A Crown Vic steered into the lot. A stern-faced woman exited, ducking under the tape, making her way toward him. She didn't look happy. "Didn't think to call your partner?"

"Thought I'd let you sleep," Jacobs replied with that winning smile, turning back to the officer and clasping a hand on his shoulder. "Good work. Write up what you have. Detective Nomura and I will take it from here."

"Oh, um, sure, let me know if you need—"

Jacobs met Nomura as she approached, pulling the gloves from her coat.

"What do we have?"

"One car. Two bikes. Three bodies. Drug deal gone bad.

Guy doing the selling met the business end of a semi." He waited. "You didn't need to come all the way down for this. Nothing to investigate."

"Then it'll be a quick investigation." Nomura walked among the wreckage. She squatted beside each downed motorcycle, turning back toward the motel. With a finger she followed the tree line, up to the road where another uniformed officer had given the signal to let traffic pass.

"Lowlife on lowlife crime," Jacobs said before his partner's mind starting getting the best of her, like it often did.

Her gaze settled on the Nissan. "Get a hit?"

"Reported stolen," he said, steering them both away from the Highway as the carload of Mexicans crept forward with the resumed flow, blending in with the rest of the merging traffic.

CHAPTER NINE

In the immediate aftermath inside the room at the Skunk Train Motor Inn, Kyle tried to focus on his breathing like the school shrink told him to do when his mom died. Slow time down, control what you can control, stay in the moment. Feel, process, move on. But how can you move on when the moment is that messed up?

He'd just seen his cousin die. Jimmy must be dead too. Leaving Kyle as the sole survivor of a shootout with the police. A hundred pounds of dope. A room full of illegal firearms. No way he was walking away from this. Fifteen, sixteen, didn't matter. Juveniles get charged as adults all the time.

None of it made sense. Why did the cops flee the scene? After Deke went down, Kyle had seen two figures exit the car, waving up a third, who came running out of the darkness, dragging the bags of weed with him and piling into the back seat. He assumed it was a man—he couldn't be sure, night so dense. Through the black fog, Kyle could only watch as they burst out of there like bandits, taillights flying up the freeway, vanishing north, fleeing the scene. What sort of cops run *away* from the scene of a crime?

Instinct took over. It wasn't his job to figure this out. You could buy one of those dashboard lights at any of the military surplus stores on the strip. He needed to get out of there. He didn't see Deke's keys so he grabbed Jimmy's. Didn't make a difference what he was driving. A stolen truck without a license was the least of his worries. He punched the F-150 in reverse and peeled out, speeding past the smoking semi jackknifed in a ditch.

At first he couldn't stop panning between the mirrors, waiting for them to be filled with police in pursuit. But those lights and sirens never came. He drove south, eyes on the road. One task at a time. Find 162. Get on the 101. Keep heading south. Autopilot. Don't ask questions. Don't think. Drive.

The sun had come up, and not thinking had become tougher to do.

Traffic on the freeway filled out, and Kyle disappeared in the glut of moving vehicles. Being just another car made him feel better, safer. He passed Ukiah, still a couple hours outside San Francisco. He needed a plan. His uncle lived in the city. He was pretty sure. San Francisco was smaller than Los Angeles, and if he could find his Uncle Joe, he'd tell him how to find his dad. Only he didn't have his uncle's address either, didn't even know what the guy looked like. But getting face time with a run-of-the-mill deadbeat had to be easier than chasing down a famous Hollywood mogul. Plus, San Fran was closer. Kyle only had the change from the burgers left, and how far could he expect to get with a few bucks? Needle threading empty, Kyle was about to find out.

He pulled off at a rest stop with a Shell station and a Jack-in-the-Box. Even though his stomach had started rumbling—he'd never gotten around to eating that burger—Kyle put all the money he had into the tank, shocked to discover how little six dollars and seventeen cents got him.

Screwing the cap back on, he spotted the brown backpack in the truck's bed, and stretched over the rail. He unzipped the bag. Then sealed it shut and scanned the grounds. Beside the comatose cashier inside, no one else was at the gas station. No other cars, no one watching. He stole another peek inside the rucksack. Stacks and stacks of hundred-dollar bills banded together.

Kyle slipped one single bill out, before stashing the resealed bag under the front seat and locking up.

He went back inside to fill up the truck. Then he headed over to Jack-in-the-Box for a bacon and egg sandwich.

Driving in his Range Rover, Scott and Lizzie shared a joint. He was a nice guy. Goofy but nice. She felt bad lying about her age and leading him to believe Chris Hansen waited on the other side of the door with a pitcher of sweet tea. But if you can't amuse yourself, what's the point?

"You know where you're going to college yet?" he asked her, re-sparking the joint that had gone out.

"The million-dollar question."

"Heard that one a few times, eh?"

"You could say that." Lizzie plucked the pot. "Have the grades and the connections to go anywhere."

"Me too. Could've gone to State or…maybe drive a cab."

Lizzie knew she sounded like a spoiled brat, bemoaning her myriad options. But she didn't bother to apologize. It was still pressure, just a different kind than most people were used to. This guy wasn't going to understand why sometimes it felt like her entire future had been etched in stone, and what *she* wanted didn't matter. As far as her father was concerned, she'd be attending Occidental College. Which was a great school, and maybe she would've been more excited if places like Brown and Stanford weren't also realistic options. She'd love to grow indignant over the injustice of it all, how unfair life was, tilted toward privilege, success nothing more than a popularity contest, but it's tough to rail against a machine tailor-made for people like you.

Still these opportunities felt more like expectations, and at times that weight proved soul crushing. Would it be so awful to take off a year to travel? Maybe go to South America with a backpack, stay in hostels, have no particular destination in mind. Trek the Camino in Spain. Sail the Mediterranean. Would it be the worst thing to work a regular job for a while?

Her parents liked to pretend they were so open-minded, so progressive. But if she were to push these ideas, they'd each have an aneurism.

"Lizzie?"

"Huh?"

"Pretty good shit, eh?" He laughed, mistaking her silence for stoned. She'd had better. "I said, you don't have *any* idea of where you want to go?"

"Turn up here. Why, Scott? You want to me to be your girlfriend?"

"I...um...we—"

"Take Twenty-fourth. I'm kidding."

"No," he protested. "I had fun last night. We should do it again. When you, you know..."

"Stop being jailbait?" Lizzie reached over and patted his hand. "Take a right on Diamond. I appreciate the offer." She pointed. "End of the block, take another right. My house is on Elizabeth."

"Lizzie's short for Elizabeth?"

"Yes, I know. My mom's named Elizabeth, too. We live on Elizabeth Street. I get it. Cute. Mine is the gleaming glass one at the end."

When they took the corner, the police cars jammed in her driveway came into view, and Scott's grip on the wheel tightened, knuckles turning white.

"Calm down. They're not here for you."

Scott slowed. "Why are cops at your house?"

"Let me out."

Scott stopped the car, and Lizzie hopped down without a goodbye.

What was this about? Not because she'd stayed out all night. Permission to do so came with her parents' blessing, albeit unspoken. What if something had happened to her mom or dad? What if there'd been a car accident? Or worse, someone had broken into their home, bludgeoned and murdered them while she was off fooling around with some frat boy. Lizzie raced up the steps.

She saw her parents right away, at the far end of the kitchen, her father seated at the table, mother gripping his shoulder, a uniformed cop and a short unattractive man, a detective of some kind, flanking them. The relief she'd felt abated as everyone's gaze settled on her.

"What's going on?"

Her father turned away, staring out the patio door, over the garden they'd just planted together.

"Mom?"

Elizabeth Decker came over and took her daughter's hand. "It's nothing, sweetheart. A misunderstanding. Why don't you go upstairs to your room?"

"To my room? I'm not a little kid." Lizzie turned to the police. They weren't giving anything away either. Not without Mom and Dad's say so. Ridiculous.

"Officer"—Lizzie leaned in and read the nameplate on his shirt—"Johnson. Will *you* please tell me what is going on?"

"Lizzie, please," her dad implored. "Can we talk about this later?"

"I want to talk about it now."

The short detective cut Lizzie off, motioning for her dad to stand up. She saw Officer Johnson reach for his handcuffs.

"You can't do this," Lizzie said, grabbing Officer Johnson's arm.

The detective removed her hand, looking up at her. "I suggest you listen to your parents."

"My parents? You mean one of whom you're arresting?"

"Jesus, Lizzie!" her father snapped—he never yelled. "I have enough to worry about. Please. We'll talk as soon as I'm back." Dave Decker turned to his wife. "Call Barry. Have him meet me down at eight-fifty Bryant." He winced a pained, apologetic smile at his daughter, before they led him away like a common criminal.

Outside half a dozen neighbors rubbernecked on their stoops, wrapped in plush bathrobes, cradling morning cups of coffee. They huddled and whispered as SFPD placed Dave Decker into the back of the cruiser. San Francisco was supposed to be the big city, but their neighborhood might as well have been in Pleasant Valley, USA, the way residents carried on, sticking their collective noses up everyone else's asses.

Lizzie slammed the door.

Her mother sat at the kitchen table, day planner and telephone out. Despite the early hour, Elizabeth Decker looked like she were preparing for a trip to the spa, perhaps a light, seasonal brunch. Lizzie wouldn't be surprised if her mother had asked to be excused during questioning so she could make herself more presentable.

Lizzie stared until her mother set down the planner.

"What?"

"What?" Lizzie repeated. "What do you think?"

Her mother exhaled and returned to her contact book, punching digits into the landline and cupping the receiver. "Now's not a good time." She effected a cool but concerned disposition. "Barry? It's Elizabeth…not so well…Dave needs you to meet him at eight-fifty Bryant…" Elizabeth stared at Lizzie. "I can't right now. But he'll explain everything when you get there…yes, now. Thanks, Barry."

When her mother hung up the phone, she let go an exaggerated exhale, stood and spun and began rifling the cupboards, casting aside organic quinoa and chia seeds. "Do you want something to eat? I'll make you breakfast. How about corn pancakes?"

Lizzie wasn't sure which part offended her more. That no one would tell her what the hell was going on, or that her mother, who couldn't boil water or toast bread, was offering to cook her breakfast, anything to avoid having a real conversation.

"You have to tell me why they took Dad, Mom. I'm not a little girl who's going to be distracted by pancakes, which, by the way, you can't even make."

Her mother whirled around. "There's been a mistake at the Foundation."

"A mistake?"

"Yes. A goddamn mistake."

"They don't arrest people for mistakes."

"Oh, grow up, Lizzie. That's *what* they arrest people for."

"So Dad made this...mistake? What did he do? Forget to take out the trash? Leave the front door open? Or does it have to do with money?"

"What would make you say that?"

"Because, Mom, I'm not a fucking idiot."

"Do not talk that way to me."

"If the guy running a charity foundation is getting picked up by the cops, it's a safe bet it has to do with money." Lizzie could see she'd touched a nerve, but her mother prided herself on never losing composure.

"I'm done talking about this. I have to help your father. So if you want to throw a tantrum, I suggest you do it elsewhere."

CHAPTER TEN

Taking the first exit off the Golden Gate Bridge, Kyle drove around until he found a twenty-four-hour Kinko's advertising internet access. Wasn't easy. Winding city streets and one-way hills deposited him downtown, which was desolate—weird, given it was the weekend.

A man in a purple shirt sat behind the counter reading a comic book. No one else was in the store.

"I need to use a computer."

"Pick one."

"Don't I have to give you money or something?"

"The instructions are on there," the man said without looking up.

Kyle didn't want to sound stupid. The only time he used computers was in the school library or at Ronnie's house. Kyle sat down at the first machine he saw. When he clicked the mouse, a screen popped up asking for a credit card.

"Hey," Kyle called to the guy. "It says I need a credit card. I don't have a credit card. I have cash."

"The machines don't work like that. You need to swipe a card. You can buy a Kinko's Card."

"Okay. Where do I buy one of those?"

The man nodded at another machine affixed to the wall. Like a coin changer at a car wash. But when Kyle made for it, the man called after him.

"Don't bother."

"Huh?"

"The machine that puts value on the card is broke."

Kyle turned back to the computer, at the busted machine on the wall, then back to the man, who still hadn't looked up from his comic. "How about I give you some money to look up a number and address for me?"

The man shook his head. "Internet's down."

"Then why would I slide my credit card?"

"The credit card you don't have? I don't know what you need the computer for. People use computers for plenty of things besides the internet." He said it like Kyle was asking how to shave a cow, as if questions don't come any dumber.

The guy returned to his comic book. Kyle walked out feeling stupid, the country boy lost in the big city. He just wanted to use a computer to find his uncle. Across the street, a pair of bums sat in front of a liquor store, rattling empty coffee cups. Kyle whisked past and bought a phone card from the cashier, who wasn't much nicer. When Kyle tried to buy a pack of cigarettes, something he had no problem doing in Dormundt, the cashier asked to see his ID, so Kyle said forget it. Kyle had never been to the city. He'd always heard how cool San Fran was. So far all he'd met were bums and jerks.

It took him almost half an hour to find a working pay phone, most of the boxes gutted with no actual phone attached.

Ronnie answered on the second ring.

"Dude, it's all over the news. What happened to your cousin?"

"What's it say on the news?"

"That he got hit by a truck and is dead. Are you all right?"

On the ground, a whole unlit cigarette lay at Kyle's feet. He picked it up and patted down his pockets but he didn't have any matches.

"Kyle?"

"Are you by a computer?"

"Yeah, why?"

"I need you to look up an address for me."

"Who?"

"Deke's dad. Joe. Joe Kelly."

Kyle could hear clacking keys. He looked up and down the street, hoping to find someone who might have a light, but downtown remained lifeless on a Saturday morning. Where was the big bustle? The city streets were as dull as Dormundt.

"There's lots of Joe Kellys," Ronnie said. "Do you have anything else? A middle name? Street?"

Kyle thought. He knew as much about his uncle as he did his dad. For a while Deke used to get mail from collection agencies looking for the guy. Kyle remembered Joe's Street. Thought it was funny a guy would live on a street named after himself.

"Try Joe's."

"Joe's? Joe on Joe's Street?"

"That's all I remember, yeah."

"Avenue? Drive?" More clacking. "No street named Joe's. You mean *Jones*?"

"Yeah, that one. What's that address?"

A man with a face like a possum sporting a nose ring passed Kyle.

"Hey, man, you have a lighter?"

The possum man said nothing, kept walking.

"Joe Kelly," Ronnie said. "214B Jones. But I think it's an old address, because—"

"Thanks. I gotta go. And Ronnie? We didn't talk."

Kyle hung up the phone. He didn't know if the police were looking for him yet. Would they be wiretapping calls? Probably not. But he wasn't staying on the phone any longer than he had to.

Back in the truck, Kyle punched the lighter but the head got stuck. Kyle reached into his pocket and retrieved Deke's pocket-knife, wedged it in the dashboard and pried the lighter out. Busted. He stuffed the knife back and dropped the unlit smoke in the ashtray to save for later.

Kyle tried to forget what Ronnie said about Deke. Of course he knew his cousin was dead, he'd seen it with his own two eyes, had heard the crunch of metal on bone, but he didn't need the confirmation. If you didn't think about the bad stuff, you could make it go away. In Dormundt, he didn't think about how few friends he had; didn't think about his mom being dead or why his dad didn't want him. If you don't think about things, it's like they're not real.

Driving over to Jones Street, the sidewalks came alive, blood-drained zombies stirring, lizard people slow to reanimate in the cold morning sun. Homeless junkies, shriveled in alleys, crawled out of filth, garbage overflowing in front of broken-down brownstone. Dirty. Diseased. Depressing.

Rolling to a stop, Kyle checked the building numbers, and found a parking spot right out front of 214. He stuffed the money deep under the seat and made sure to lock both doors. You didn't need to grow up in the big city to tell this wasn't the kind of neighborhood where you left doors unlocked.

Kyle climbed the steps and checked the boxes. The only name listed next to 214B was for a K. Johnson. He pushed the button anyway. The intercom crackled.

"What do you want?" a woman's voice barked.

"I'm looking for my uncle."

"What? Huh?"

"My uncle. I'm looking—"

The intercom cut off.

Kyle waited a couple seconds, tugged at the gate, but when it remained locked he buzzed again.

He heard an upstairs door slam a few moments later, followed by heavy breathing and footsteps clomping down the steps.

A large woman appeared at the door, face like a battered catcher's mitt, meaty hands big as one too. She didn't open the gate. "What you want? Why you keep ringing my bell first thing on a Saturday morning?"

"I'm looking for my uncle."

"Who the hell's your uncle?"

"Joe Kelly."

"He don't live here." The woman started back upstairs.

"Please."

The woman stopped and turned around. "How old are you?"

"What's it matter?"

"You look twelve."

"I'm not. I'm old enough to drive." Kyle dangled the keys.

She wrinkled her mouth and shook her big head, then pushed open the metal gate. "He ain't lived here a while. But I think I have some old mail upstairs. C'mon."

Kyle ducked inside and closed the grate, relieved to leave behind the dirty city streets.

He wasn't relieved for long.

The inside of the apartment was just as dirty—unwashed plates and takeout cartons dripping sauces and meaty juices, the ripe smell of unwashed funk. The whole place stank like greasy fried food and feet. Kyle had never done more than smoked pot, but he'd been around plenty of people who did the harder shit, too, enough to know the telltale signs. He spied lighters and blackened glass stems, strips of scorched aluminum foil.

"Where you from?" the big woman asked.

"Why?"

"'Cause you ain't from the city, honey."

"Actually, I do live in the city. On the other side."

"Uh huh."

There were sticker books on the table, and toys spread over the filthy floor. Maybe they belonged to someone she babysat. Didn't make a difference. Kids shouldn't be around this stuff.

The woman lit a cigarette and leaned inside a doorframe, terrycloth bathrobe parting to reveal a thick, mottled thigh. Kyle didn't like the way she was looking at him.

"What you so nervous for?"

"I'm not nervous."

"Then sit down. Relax. I ain't gonna bite."

A door opened behind him and a skinny boy, pants hanging off his butt and no shirt, came strutting out. He couldn't have been much older than Kyle, but the way he carried himself he seemed a lot older.

"Who the fuck is this?" he said, not looking at Kyle as he swiped a shirt off the radiator.

"You're gonna be late," the woman said.

Two seconds later a little kid, four or five, toddled out and ran to the woman and gave her a hug. She kissed the top of his head and patted his behind.

"Come on," the boy called to the little kid, who followed after him, oblivious to Kyle's presence, as if strange dudes showed up all day long.

Brother? He wasn't old enough to be his father.

After they left the woman waddled into her kitchen, abandoning Kyle in the messy room. Cityscape sounds bled up from the street, buses grinding, ambulances wailing, crazies shouting with unhinged laughter. Kyle felt his entire body tense. He could sure use a toke. He half expected the front door to kick open and that skinny boy, whoever he was, to come back in, guns blasting. Maybe he didn't need to get high; he was already paranoid. Then again, after last night, such violence didn't seem so fantastic anymore.

The big lady returned with a stack of envelopes. He fanned through them. Utility bills, cable bills, all addressed to his uncle at this address.

"What's this?"

"Kept sending those bills even after I told them the man don't live here. They pretty old though."

"What do you want me to do with them?"

"How should I know? You the one who came here looking for him."

"I need to know where he is living, like, now."

"He's *your* uncle! Call PG&E!"

Kyle scratched his head. "Can I use your phone?"

The big woman huffed. "Over there." She pointed to a tiny table by the window. "Make it quick. It's only toll-free calls. So don't be chatting up your girlfriend in Las Vegas."

He lifted the receiver. Then put it back down. "What am I supposed to say?"

"Jesus Christ. You are helpless." She stomped over and snatched the phone out of his hand.

Kyle stood there as the woman squawked at an operator for ten minutes, something about being a landlord and having old mail she needed to forward to the former tenant, and no matter how many times whoever was on the other end protested or resisted, the woman wasn't hanging up until she got the information she wanted and Kyle needed—a scribbled address in L.A. on the back of one of those delinquent bills. Kyle folded the envelope and stuck it in his back pocket, leaving the rest of the stack.

At the door he turned around to say thanks, but she cut him off.

"I don't know what you're doing here. But you better go back home, honey." Despite the term of endearment, it wasn't a warm wish. "This place gonna eat you up." She slammed the door.

Descending the dark stairwell, which reeked of cleaning chemicals and oily car parts, Kyle pulled the utility bill and read the address again. Echo Park? How long had his uncle been in Los Angeles? Was that why he and Deke stopped talking? Maybe his uncle moved in with his dad. He wished Deke were around so he could ask him this stuff.

Kyle heard the hydraulics before he saw the tow truck.

"What are you doing?" he screamed, running outside, down the steps.

"You parked in a white zone."

Kyle stared down at the curb. The back of the truck extended into the white area maybe three, five feet, tops.

"I'll move it."

"Too late." The red Ford F-150 was already hitched.

"C'mon, man."

"Kid, once it's on the hook, nothing I can do about it. Gotta pay to get it down."

"Fine. How much?"

The tow truck driver gave the chain a final tug to make sure it was secure. "Gotta ask the impound yard."

"How about I just pay you?"

"Don't work like that."

"I'll pay you twice as much. Cash. Right now."

"I said it don't work like that." The tow truck driver climbed in his cab.

"At least let me get my stuff out." Kyle sprinted back to the truck and jumped for the handle, but it was too high.

The driver bear hugged him from behind, pulling him down. "What you think you're doing?"

"I need to get my bag!"

The driver shoved Kyle on his ass. "Try that shit again, I'm calling the cops."

That was the last thing Kyle needed. He had no choice but to watch the tow truck drive away with all the money.

CHAPTER ELEVEN

Lizzie knew Melanie would be at Dragonfly. They met Brenda and Jax for brunch there every weekend, the upscale sidewalk café having no problem serving seventeen-year-olds mimosas.

The lower half of Twenty-fourth Street ran through the heart of Little Mexico, which boasted plenty of local, ethnic flavor—colorful street murals, authentic cuisine, Mariachi music—but wretchedness and poverty still lurked on every corner in the flats. Tough hombres lay passed out behind rough-and-tumble barrio bars. Dealers slipped balloons from their mouths like poorly kept secrets. A few short blocks up the hill however, in swanky, gentrified Noe Valley, the preferred neighborhood of yuppie families and tiny dogs, Twenty-fourth Street played more like a cozy college town boulevard, blocks peppered with specialty shops—Tibetan scarves, hand-whittled rocking chairs, pottery thrown by bored housewives with disposable income because sales from lopsided mugs couldn't even cover a week's rent in this district let alone turn a profit. There were bars on the hill too, but alcoholism in Noe Valley wasn't a career; it was kitsch.

Lizzie had hoped to talk to Melanie about what was happening with her dad. Once her friends spotted her, she knew that wouldn't be possible. The catcalls started from halfway up the block.

"Take a seat, playa," Melanie said, kicking out a chair.

Jax leaned over to sip his mimosa. "It's OK, girl. I had my

own walk of shame this morning."

Everyone laughed. Lizzie didn't get the joke, which meant she either missed the backstory, or it wasn't funny.

"I don't know why you're being so secretive now," Melanie said. "You molested the poor guy last night."

"Melanie told us he goes to State?"

"We're like twinsies," Jax said as he picked around his goat cheese and arugula omelet. "I had a college boy too. What was yours called?"

"I don't feel like talking about it."

"Did something happen?" Melanie scooched closer, ears perked, excited. She feasted off potential drama.

At that moment, Lizzie hated all her friends.

A waiter approached and everyone stopped talking. "Can I get you anything?" Neat black vest, button-down, clean-shaven and moisturized. All the waiters at Dragonfly looked like they'd just stepped out of a *GQ* spread. "Mimosa?"

"No, thanks."

"I'll take another," chimed Melanie, cuing Brenda and Jax, who both nodded. "Make it four."

"Three," said Lizzie.

"Fine," Melanie said. "Three. And the check." She waited until the waiter left. "Who's coming with me to Now and Zen today?"

"Can't. Have to go with the parents to San Jose. Grandma is undergoing the chemo." Jax mimicked sticking his finger down his throat.

"I'm out too," Brenda said. "Yoga. Then babysitting my sister's kid while they go house shopping."

"They're buying *another* house?"

"Flipping."

It was then Lizzie understood why she despised her friends so much. It was the act, insincere. Like extras on *Gossip Girl*, outtakes from a *Vogue* article concerning the disaffected kids of affluence, an audition for another unnecessary reality show about privileged, vapid teens. The way Jax inserted the word "the" in front of certain nouns, expressing his grandmother's dying as little more than inconvenience; the way Brenda felt the need to combine "yoga" with "house flipping." They were immature imposters playing make-believe in a fantasized grown-up world.

"You're still coming, right?" Melanie asked her.

Radio stations often sponsored free concerts in Golden Gate Park. KFOG's Now and Zen featured a bunch of indie bands that Lizzie liked. She'd been planning on going all week. Except now the thought of standing around a crowded, muddy field with thrift store hipsters and bankers letting loose made Lizzie want to retch.

"I don't know. Can we talk about it later?"

"Great," Melanie said. "You're flaking."

The waiter brought the mimosas and the check. Which Melanie used as an excuse to embarrass Lizzie.

"Do *you* want to come with me to a concert?" Melanie asked him. "Because apparently my best friend in the world is too busy. Even though she *told* me, weeks in advance, that she'd go. And now it's too late to get someone else. Which fucks up my *whole* weekend—"

"Jesus Christ. All right. I'll go."

Jax made a show of hoisting his boho crocheted bag to the table. Lizzie loved the gay boys. She was friends with several. She lived in San Francisco, after all. But Jax also had to push everything to the limit. It wasn't like he needed to carry a purse; Jax refused to use a wallet because "that's what those breeder boys" do, turning storing credit cards into a political statement. Jax slipped out a twenty, pecked another teeny bird sip, leaving most of his refreshed mimosa untouched.

"You can finish that if you want," he said to Lizzie.

"I'm okay, thanks."

"What's gotten into you, Debbie Downer?" Melanie prodded.

"She doesn't like to kiss and tell," Jax said. "Leave her alone."

"I'm just tired." Lizzie had come down here because she thought talking about her father's arrest would alleviate the anxiety. The visit had produced the opposite result.

"I dated at guy from State last fall," Brenda said.

Cars, all looking the same, cruised past. Young, attractive mothers, with the kinds of bounce-back baby bodies only money can buy, pushed accessorized strollers between the bakeries and boutiques. Through a field of cocked plaid hats and ironic mustaches, granola warriors pedaled their sustainable bicycles beyond the free trade coffee bodegas. This whole strip of Twenty-fourth, like the rest of Lizzie's world, a make-believe bubble.

"I told him I wasn't ready for anything serious," Brenda said. "It didn't work out."

Jax stood and tucked his extra small tee tighter, then leaned over his flute. "Maybe one more sip for the road."

He squeezed Lizzie's arm and whispered in her ear, "Relax, honey. Whatever it is, it can't be that bad."

You have no idea.

Richter detective Ray Carter sat in the passenger seat, watching the EMTs clean up last night's mess. He reached into the take-out bag and pulled out a fistful of sweet and sour packets. He tore off the tops with his teeth and squirted a gob onto a cold egg roll, smearing it with his finger like a butter knife. He bit into congealed pork and cabbage, squinching his face like he'd teeted curdled milk.

The driver's side door opened and his partner, Earl Banks, climbed in and tossed a greasy paper sack onto Carter's lap.

"What this?"

"Lunch."

Carter wadded up the egg roll wrapper and chucked it to the floor. He rifled through the bag. "Great. Big improvement. A pair of cold hamburgers."

"All that was in the room. Clerk was useless. Fucking hippy

was so high, he didn't know what planet he was on."

"How'd you get past Dormundt's finest?"

"Don't worry I didn't use my real name. Flash a badge down here and mention a big town and they roll out the red carpet. So damned thrilled to stand next to a real cop."

"Real cop," Carter muttered. "For how long?"

Across the street, uniforms directed rubberneckers to keep moving. Unshaven, middle-aged men in sweats and grubby tees, beer bellies bobbing over belts, sat in plastic chairs outside their doors, swilling cheap brew from ice buckets, watching the action unfold. For them, it was just another TV show, albeit with better acting and crisper picture.

"How long you think we can duck Captain Sturgis?" Banks said.

"Not long."

"We're doing our jobs."

"This far out of our jurisdiction? Sturgis is a good ol' boy. But he's not stupid. We didn't draw the long straw. It's Cutting's baby."

"You saw how long Cutting stuck around. Him and that bitch couldn't get out of here fast enough."

"We're hands off," Carter reiterated.

"We're still cops."

"In name only. Just a matter of time till someone notices that cash is missing, puts two and two together. Internal affairs is already up our asses." Carter stared over at his partner. "I think a little personal time is in order. Leave a message with the captain, say we got a lead, then we ditch the phones. We come back with the goods, we're heroes, and no one is the wiser."

Carter lit a cigarette and studied the scene across the Highway, the placement of the bodies and bikes in juxtaposition to the room. Of course they didn't check in using their real names, even a couple low level potheads couldn't be that brain dead. Then again, they were willing to unload a hundred pounds of dope for dimes on the dollar through a screw-up fence like Chip

Morsman. Hell, maybe it was their fault. Should've left well enough alone. After the bust the other night, they had plenty of schwag to turn a nifty profit. Everything would've been copacetic, too, if those fucking bikers hadn't crashed the party. Didn't matter now. He and Banks had one choice: get that cash back in to the evidence room or kiss their asses goodbye. The clock was already ticking down.

"What about Morsman?" Banks asked.

"Fuck him."

"What about Jacobs?"

"Fuck him, too."

"There's no other way? We can't unload what we got?"

"That kind of volume? This fast with this kind of heat? That's why bills are photographed and serialed." Carter pointed across the Highway at the Skunk Train. "We're on our own here. We need *that* cash back. We take this shit underground. I'm talking DL, off the radar." He lowered his eyes to convey this wasn't up for debate. "Agreed?"

Banks nodded. "What's our next move?"

"Returning to the scene of the crime is cliché and flashing badges is amateur hour." Carter stared at the cold burgers in his lap. "Dollars to donuts, these came from the Ironside, only place that serves burgers around here, which I'll bet is how Cord Eason and his boy knew this was going down. My guess is somebody got the munchies and made a midnight run. Let's go see who was hungry."

CHAPTER TWELVE

Caked in mud like a *National Geographic* bushman, Jimmy squatted in the scrub brush on the fringes of school grounds, waiting for Kristy, Deke's ex, to come out. He seethed with murderous intent over what he'd do to Kyle when he caught up with him.

After Deke met the business end of that tractor trailer and those crooked cops split the scene, Jimmy could only watch from his spot deep in the woods as that little shit, Kyle, stole his truck—and his money.

Jimmy used the heavy forest as cover, skirting the fringes of town through the Dormundt swamps. Wilfred Elementary was two miles from the motel, but Jimmy made the mistake of checking Kristy's house first. Should've known she'd be at work on her day off. Kristy possessed that annoying trait of wanting to make the world a better place.

Even someone as dumb as Kyle had to realize the deep shit he was in by now, and chances were, he was already hightailing it south. Kid never shut up about finding Daddy in Hollywood. But he might've contacted Kristy first. Jimmy had seen Deke toss the backpack. He doubted Kyle could have seen that from the room. The kid had no reason to look in the bed. Both good and bad news. If Kyle didn't know what he had, he couldn't blow the money. But it also meant a hundred grand was sitting out in the open. The cops had been too distracted by the fire-fight to get the money back. The pigs would figure it out soon enough. That is, if Kyle didn't stumble upon it first.

There were only three cars in the school parking lot. Jimmy didn't want to risk running into a do-gooder principal or some nerd who spent his weekends eavesdropping on police scanners in the library. So he waited. Even though doing so gave Kyle one helluva head start.

Around noon the school doors pushed open, and Kristy made her way toward the Civic. Jimmy caught up with her as she was inserting the key. He held a finger to his mouth, pointing at the passenger's side.

"What are you doing here, Jimmy? And why are you covered in mud?"

He lit a cigarette.

"Please don't smoke in my car."

Jimmy blew out a ring. "Drive."

"You want to tell me where we're going?" Kristy flipped her directional as she shifted into gear.

"Go the other way."

Kristy turned left. "Okay. Now can you—"

"Deke's dead."

"What?"

"Got hit by a truck this morning. We were in the middle of a dope deal. It was a setup. I took off into the woods. He was running along the Highway. Tractor trailer hit him."

"You're positive that he's—"

"If he ain't dead, honey, he's sure gonna be walking funny. Truck was going at least seventy. Hit him square on"—Jimmy smacked one hand against the other—"split him six ways to Sunday."

Kristy took a moment. "Does Kyle know?"

"Little shit was there."

"Oh my God. Is he okay?"

Jimmy scanned the quiet, tree-lined Dormundt streets. Nothing seemed suspicious. Jimmy had a pretty good sixth sense about this shit.

"Do you know where he is?"

"Kyle?" Jimmy said. "Last time I seen him? Driving my truck." Jimmy eyeballed her. "You wouldn't be lying to me?"

"About what?"

"Not having talked to Kyle?"

"Why would I have talked to Kyle?"

"I don't know who else he'd come running to. I need to find him."

"Because he has your truck?"

"He has a lot more than that." Jimmy pointed ahead. "Loop around and drop me off at the truck stop on the north end of the Highway. I need to shower and catch a ride."

"Where are you going?"

Jimmy didn't answer. He had to think. If Kristy wasn't lying, and she didn't appear to be—he'd been around enough women to know when a bitch was lying—he'd trust his gut.

"We need to call the police."

"Fuck the police. Didn't you hear me? I said we were ass deep in the middle of a dope deal."

"Kyle too?"

"Fuck yeah. He's a part of this. You care about that little shit, you keep your mouth shut."

"What are you going to do when you find him?"

"I ain't gonna hurt him, if that's what you mean."

"Your word?"

"Yes, Kristy, you have my word. I just want back what belongs to me. You have any way of getting ahold of his father?"

"You think that's where he's going?"

"Where else?"

Kristy shook her head. "Nobody does."

"One more thing—don't talk to the cops."

"Yes, you already made that clear."

"No. You don't understand. They were there last night. They bolted after they shot and killed a couple bikers. These weren't regular cops."

"What do you mean?"

"They were the ones buying the dope."

"Undercover?"

"I don't think so. That scumbag Chip Morsman might know the score. He helped arrange the sale. But I don't have time to track him down right now. I'll deal with him later. All I know is real cops would've stuck around."

"What are you trying to say?"

"I'm not *trying* to say anything. One of two possibilities: they weren't real cops, or they were dirty. Either way, you can't trust the police right now. You want to help Kyle? Then help me find him. He's in way over his head. He's carrying a lot of cash stashed in my truck, which he may or may not know about. It's the sort of money people go looking for."

"What kind of people?"

"The kind you don't want finding you."

The impound address was tacked on a lamppost. Kyle doled out change to a street person for directions and tried to remain positive. He knew he had a tendency to let things snowball.

Dormundt bored Kyle to death, but right now he'd give anything to be back in his weed-filled backyard fiddling with rusted car parts, waiting for Deke to come home and yell at him.

Kyle sprinted across the intersection of Market and Van Ness and hooked a left onto Howard, aiming for Seventh and Harrison. He passed a trio of grubby-looking street urchins giving him the eye. He pushed open the doors to the AutoReturn office.

"Can I help you?" the man behind a plexiglass window asked.

"I need to get my truck."

"Then you're going to have to give us some money." He laughed.

"How much?"

"Depends how long we've had it."

"Like half hour, tops. I was up on Jones. I went to see my, um, friend, and I parked a teeny bit in the white—like this much." Kyle pinched his finger and thumb together. "And some truck driver towed it—"

"If you parked in a no parking zone, even this much"—the man mimicked Kyle's pinching—"you're going to get towed." The man pressed a single key. "Standard retrieval charge is four hundred and fifty-two dollars—"

"Four hundred and fifty what?"

"For the first four hours, which are a courtesy—"

"Courtesy?"

"That doesn't include the cost of the violation. That's fifty-six twenty-five for the first twenty-four hours, and another sixty-two seventy-five, per day, after that."

Kyle didn't need to add up what he had in his pocket. "The thing is," he said leaning in, "my…money…is in the truck."

The man smirked. "Now, that *is* a problem, because everything in that truck belongs to the city of San Francisco until you pay the fine."

Kyle knew the man was mocking him but there was nothing he could do about it.

A stout woman barged through the door, toting a crying baby in a car seat, tapping her foot, groaning.

"Come back when you get the money, son. We'll be here." He looked past his shoulder at the woman and crying baby. "Next."

Detective Jacobs sat at his desk in the Cutting precinct, files from recent narco cases stacked high, arrest records spread before him, trying to sort out the Skunk Train aftermath. He needed to get the official report straight. By now he had the deceased's name, Declan Kelly, as well as that of his associate, James McDermott. Kelly's truck had been left at the scene. McDermott's, however, was missing. Kelly didn't have a record, but McDermott had had plenty of run-ins with the law. Assaults and batteries, drunk and disorderlies, bar fights. A real piece of work. Never did more than a week or two in county. No family, no place to hide out. Jacobs wasn't worried about McDermott. Dumb hick like him would trip up. Jacobs was more concerned about the kid. Declan Kelly's fifteen-year-old cousin, Kyle Gill. All three had been at the Skunk Train Inn. After the shootout, guests reported seeing a boy drive off in a red truck. When police later searched the room, they discovered the gunnysack stuffed with AK-47s, sawed-off shotguns, and automatics. Turns out the Skunk Train bloodbath could've been a whole lot bloodier.

Nomura strolled to his desk.

"What are you doing here?" he said. "I told you I got this. It's Saturday. Go home, get some sleep. Trust me, this nightmare will be here Monday. Not sure what more you can do."

"How about I give you the names of the two cops at the Skunk Train last night?" Detective Nomura wrinkled her mouth.

Jacobs pushed his chair back, hands behind his head. "I'm listening."

"There was a seizure three nights ago. Couple hundred pounds of marijuana. Between Cutting and Richter. Never logged into evidence."

Jacobs waited. Nomura knew his next question, but she was going to make him ask anyway.

"If there's no record, we know this how?"

"The man who the pot belonged to, Chip Morsman, called it in."

"A drug dealer reported...a robbery?"

"Morsman claims the cops stole his dope, and then wanted his help buying more in exchange for not charging him. Were planning on flipping it."

"To whom?"

"Whoever pays the most during a shortage? Highest bidder."

Jacobs shook his head. "We're supposed to take the word of a dope dealer? Where'd you hear this?"

"Andy Williams, sheriff in Dormundt."

"Why are you talking to Dormundt? I'm lead on this."

"Trying to stay ahead of the curve," Nomura said. "This Morsman is known around town as a real fuck-up."

"Who in that town *isn't* a fuck-up?" Jacobs creased his brow. "Not our concern. Sounds like Dormundt's problem."

"Except Morsman claimed he helped set up the deal at the Skunk Train last night."

When Jacobs transferred from LAPD, he'd taken a helluva hit on salary. But the job came with perks. Cherry-picked caseload, less risk of gang retaliation. He was also told he'd be working alone, which is how he liked it. Then after he'd given up his rent-controlled apartment on the Santa Monica Pier, packed all his belongings, and made the move, they'd dumped this Nomura on him. She wasn't a bad detective. But like most in law enforcement up here, she'd seen too many cop shows. He didn't have time for show-and-tell.

"Where's Morsman now?"

"No one knows. He called this morning, said he heard about the Skunk Train on the news and was worried his life was in danger. Thinks these cops are going come after him. When Williams tried to secure a location, he hung up. Dormundt PD is out looking for him now."

Jacobs grabbed his files, stacked them in a row, lined up the edges, a compulsive habit. Or maybe it was a coping mechanism to not blow a gasket.

"Until they find him," he said, "I'm not sure I'm willing to take the word of a drug dealer."

"Ray Carter and Earl Banks."

Jacobs arched his brow. Every once in a while, someone surprised him.

"Detectives over in Richter. Know 'em?"

"Why would I?" He paused, smiling. He twiddled his fingers. "Come on, Nomura, don't hold out on your partner. What else aren't you telling me?"

"Only that IA is investigating them."

"For?"

"Drugs and money missing from evidence. Brutality charges. Repeated pattern. They are well known for their brand of good ol' boy renegade justice."

"And you think these two are the cops we're looking for because they have a bad reputation?"

"Ricardo Ruiz, internal affairs. He's an old…friend."

The way she said it, Jacobs knew this Ruiz was more than "a friend." Internal affairs didn't divulge information to the rank and file, especially when narcotics were involved. Jacobs had pegged Nomura as a climber the minute they met.

"I called him," Nomura continued, "to see if he had anyone who might fit the bill. I'm telling you, these two are tailor-made."

Jacobs leaned back and eyed Nomura. If she were right, this would prove a boon for her career. More importantly it would save his. The move to Dormundt hadn't been the cakewalk he was hoping for. No doubt it was a stretch. But it had legs. With the right man running the show.

Like she was reading his mind, she said, "I know. No one is rushing to accuse a pair of cops, even ones in hot water with IA. But we have two narcotics officers under investigation, a cop car spotted at the crime scene last night, and now Morsman's allegations."

"Where are our Mr. Carter and Mr. Banks now?"

"Captain Sturgis in Richter is asking the same question. They've gone radio silent. Left a message they were following a lead, and to charge them personal time. Said they'd be back in a few days."

"Interesting." Jacobs got up and snared his coat from the back of his chair, sliding in an arm.

"Where are you going?"

"Back down to Dormundt, see if we can smoke Chip Morsman out of his hole. I'd like to find out what the hell two police officers were doing in the middle of a drug deal with stolen evidence." Before she could ask, he added, "No, I don't need any company. But since you won't take my advice and get some sleep, do me a favor and see what you can find on Kyle Gill."

"Who's he?"

"Fifteen-year-old kid who was at the Skunk Train last night."

Nomura's face twisted up. "What's he got to do with all this?"

"That's what I'd like to find out."

CHAPTER THIRTEEN

Standing on the sidewalk, surrounded by shuffling homeless and pedestrians, Kyle fought to keep his emotions in check. A few hours ago, he'd had all that money, sitting there, his, to do with whatever he pleased, and now here he was, in a strange city, broke, with nowhere to go, no one to ask for help, and in all likelihood wanted by the authorities.

When Kyle got in trouble at school, they made him talk to the school shrink, who said he lashed out because he'd lost his parents at such a young age; he was worried about losing other things too. What a joke. He hadn't lost his dad. He told her that his father was busy making movies, which was a helluva lot more important than talking to troublemakers and losers at a high school. The shrink said he should come back when he calmed down. He never did.

Now he realized the doctor had been right. What would stop the rest of his world from falling apart? What would prevent him from ending up like these filthy bastards drinking out of paper bags and crapping their pants? He'd never seen so many homeless people. Tents. Sleeping bags. Cardboard boxes rearranged into makeshift apartments that an asthmatic wolf could blow down. Maybe this is how it happened. One day, the city swallowed you up, and there'd be no one to pull you out, and you disappeared, left to join the invisible masses.

"Hey," someone shouted.

A dirty white boy with gnarled yellow dreads, pierced nose,

ears, and lip, slinked toward him. Kyle recognized him as one of the gutter punks outside the tow yard. He could smell the kid from five feet away. The sleeveless jean jacket he wore over his hoodie was so crusty it almost shone, as if the grime had somehow been pressed and polished, showcasing a slick, oily sheen. When the kid stuck out his hand, Kyle flinched, expecting a punch. But the kid extended a burning joint instead. Right there in broad daylight. He didn't care. Kyle never needed to get high more.

"Fuckers steal your car?" the kid asked but didn't give Kyle a chance to answer. "They call it towing, but it ain't towing, man. It's stealing. You can't afford to get it out, because they charge, like, a thousand bucks a day, and they know it, man, that's why they take cars from people who can't get them out, see? It's a racket. Then they sell them at private auctions, make the city a nice profit. Fucking fascists."

Kyle hit the joint again, a warm, mellow high descending like eiderdown.

"Raf," the gutter punk said, offering a fist. He pointed up the block at two more street kids dressed alike, tattered denim, matted hair, sunburnt homeless faces, one ratted and tiny, the other a great big fat guy who could pass for thirty. "That's Scabby Shea and Big Wes."

They nodded back.

"What's your name?" Raf asked, relieving him of the pot.

"Kyle."

"You don't live in the city, do you, Kyle?"

Kyle shook his head. Scabby Shea and Big Wes loafed over with toted bedrolls under their arms. Up close, Kyle could see why they called him Scabby; his face was pitted with cavernous acne craters the size of nickels.

You got any plans?" Raf asked.

"Find a way to get my truck?"

"Standing around ain't gonna help you do that." Raf passed him back the joint. "Listen, I know a guy who might be able to help."

"For real?"

"I wouldn't bullshit you. He's a cool dude, has plenty of cash. He's helped me out of jams before. The thing is, he won't be around till tonight so I can't ask him till then. In fact, I'm supposed to see him later on. Got a house up in the hills. You can come with and talk to him. Can't promise anything." Raf tilted his head. "You got money where you're from? He's a cool dude, but he's not going to *give* you the money."

"I can pay him back. I have money in the truck. But they won't let me get it."

Raf slapped him on the shoulder. "Then you got nothing to worry about. Long as you can pay him back, fucking guy will drive you down here."

"What's in it for him?"

"Nothing, man. Like I said. He's a cool dude." Raf bobbed his dreaded head. "So now what you doing?"

"Nothing, I guess."

"We're about to head up to the park. Free concert this weekend."

This kid might've been full of it, but right now he was the best chance Kyle had to get the truck out. The only other person Kyle could think of asking for help, Ronnie, freaked out over anything involving money. Ronnie's house was on The Arlington, where all the wealthy families in Dormundt lived. You couldn't ask people like that for favors. Especially favors involving their money. Poor people will give you the shirt off their back. The rich ones? Lucky if you get their leftovers.

"Let's go," Kyle said.

"Cool. You got any cigarettes?"

Thousands flooded Golden Gate Park, the grounds swelling with young and old alike, the respectable and destitute. Stylish couples pushed strollers with babies sporting mohawks. Modern savages raged against commerce while the liberated businessmen grooved like it was 1967 all over again. Vendor booths and food trucks defined the border, folding tables under nylon canopies hawking native dishes, screen-printed tees and hand-knitted beanies. Amnesty International and PETA volunteers waved clipboards to sign.

An opening act onstage, two girls with a banjo and drum machine, harmonized a song about going home. Aside from a few hippy chicks swaying in flowing flowery dresses, no one was paying much attention until the bands that mattered went on later. Police in pairs patrolled through the haze of marijuana smoke.

Lizzie hadn't stopped back home, hadn't even checked her cell. Even though she was worried about her father, she felt too angry, too betrayed to get an update. All he had to say was he didn't do it. And he couldn't even look her in the eye.

"Well?" Melanie asked, tugging Lizzie's arm.

Lizzie stared, expressionless.

"Have you heard a word I said?"

"No. I haven't. I tried to tell you back at Dragonfly. It's been a bad day."

The comment didn't register with Melanie, who nodded past her shoulder.

"Look over there."

Lizzie started to turn.

Melanie spun her back. "Don't be so obvious. It's that guy, Trevor. From Carousel. Like, two months ago? He had the friend you liked. Mike. Matt. Or...something with an M. I forget. But you *really* liked him."

Lizzie had no recollection of the night in question, the guy or the club, but in that moment she doubted she could feel much of anything for anyone.

As they headed up Haight Street, Kyle noted the wide swath people cut, tilting their noses and turning away, as if they feared getting infected by the approaching scourge. Instead of being shamed, though, the boys championed their undesirable mantle, held their heads high, stomping their oversized boots in defiance. These kids had balls. Kyle had always felt like a second-class citizen up in Dormundt, in particular around rich friends like Ronnie. He'd been ashamed of Deke's dumpy house, of not being able to afford a car and having to pedal a bicycle to get around town, and here were these street punks with nothing but the filthy clothes on their backs, strutting up the street with safety pins protruding from their eyebrows like they owned the place.

"You have, like, a job?" Kyle asked. He felt stupid before the question was out of his mouth, and he felt worse after the way the others stifled giggles, as though pitying the little boy who still believed in magic.

"Fuck that shit. Might as well be a dead man." Raf stopped. "I'd rather *be* dead, man. Show up at a goddamn factory every day, drive a bus, mop up someone else's shit? For what? Minimum wage? Make more than that out here."

Kyle didn't want to ask how exactly and risk getting ridiculed again.

Raf slung an arm around his shoulder. "Don't worry. Hang with us. We'll show you how it's done."

The pack of boys crossed in front of a liquor store and approached Golden Gate Park. All three plopped down on the sidewalk without a word. Big Wes ripped a piece of cardboard from his tattered rucksack and propped it up by his big, booted feet. The hand-scrawled message: "Ain't Gonna Lie, Need To Get Drunk."

Kyle remained standing, as the others peeled off their grimy hoodies and raked fingers through matted hair. Another day at the office. Scabby Shea set out a grubby coffee cup, stained from dirt and copper pennies.

"What are you doing?"

"What's it look like?" Raf said. "Need money for beer. Can't go listen to music if you're not at least buzzed."

People walked past, most refusing to look down, the few who did harboring expressions between mild disgust and outright scorn. Three feet away lay a bum who smelled like he'd soiled himself.

"How much do you need?" Kyle asked.

Raf gazed up, squinting from the sun. "For what?"

"To get the beer?"

Raf scratched his scruffy beard as if he had to do some serious math. "Six, seven bucks."

Kyle pulled out the few bills he had left. "Here's ten."

Raf nodded at Big Wes, who clearly did the buying since he looked at least a dozen years older than the rest.

Big Wes pushed himself up and snagged the money, ducking inside. Moments later he returned with three forty-ounce bottles concealed in brown paper bags. The three boys raised the beer in a toast to Kyle, who couldn't hide the goofy grin on his face for having done something right.

The music bled through the wall of trees blocks away, washing down the street in a wave of screeching distortion, pounding drums, and a choir of indiscernible voices. The boys traded swigs. Mixed with the little bit of shake they had left, Kyle was feeling all right.

"Who's playing?" Kyle asked, not that it mattered. Ronnie was always showing off some new band he'd heard about. Deke listened to the same stuff his buddy Jimmy did, old-school outlaw country. If it wasn't on the radio, Kyle didn't know about it.

"Bunch of bullshit," Scabby Shea said.

"Bunch of bands, man," said Big Wes. "Indie, some straight-up rock."

"Nerd music," Scabby Shea corrected.

"Don't listen to him," said Raf, as they trounced over park grass, Doc Martens doing serious damage. "If it's not screamcore, he don't listen to it."

"Fuck that shit," said Scabby Shea. "It's called grindcore. Stop calling it screamcore. That's emo bullshit."

Kyle had no idea what they were talking about. If he admitted the only CD he owned was by Bruce Springsteen, they'd laugh his ass all the way back to Dormundt. But Kyle liked Springsteen. Every time he sang that song about getting out of a town full of losers, Kyle would crank it up. Yeah, he might be nothing now but one day he'd prove everyone wrong.

As the boys entered the concert grounds, the wide, green expanse of the park splayed open. Place was packed. Young dudes with tiny mustaches and tight jeans, ugly sweaters and hats from the 1940s. And girls. So many pretty girls it made your heart ache. On their phones, texting and talking, leaning on each other, laughing like they'd just heard the best joke in the world.

There were a lot of other gutter punks, all looking the same as Raf and his crew. Jean jackets with the sleeves cut off, hooded sweatshirts, layers of rank tees, and pink, puffy faces. The uniform of the street soldier. Raf seemed to know them all.

Bottles passed back and forth, joints too, right out in the open, cops strolling by and not saying a word.

Kyle's head buzzed with a million grayhead flies, the memory of last night and what happened to Deke being pushed further down, hidden from conscious consideration. It was the perfect state. Not too wasted that he couldn't function. But buzzed enough that he didn't have to deal with the unpleasant stuff.

Or maybe he was too high. Because why else was that pretty girl staring at him? And why was she smiling like that? She was standing with another girl and some older guys, grown-up versions of jocks back home, the kind of guys Kyle would always hate. But she wasn't looking at them. She was looking at him. He peeked to make sure there wasn't a giant clock over his head. Then the girl looked away, concealing a coy, flirty grin, like she'd been caught doing something naughty, which made Kyle's face flush and heart beat fast.

CHAPTER FOURTEEN

"Nice going," Melanie said after Lizzie turned back around.

"Huh?"

"You didn't say two words to them."

"Who?"

"Um. The three cute guys that had been standing here, talking to us for the last ten minutes? Or I should say, talking to *me*, because you have your head in lala land. Why are you blushing? What the hell is wrong with you today? I've been trying…"

Melanie's voice droned on and Lizzie let the music drown it out. The girl was in love with the sound of her own voice. All she talked about was boys. Empty-headed, emotionally stunted, boring Polo-shirt types destined to work in high finance, potential husbands to feed her lies about needing to work late and Las Vegas conventions. And the saddest part? Melanie would happily swallow it all in exchange for unlimited credit. Sometimes Lizzie couldn't remember what made them best friends in the first place. She'd grown as sick of Melanie as she had the rest of her life. Seventeen years old and already fed up with everything.

If Lizzie had overheard someone her age inside, say, a Starbucks, dressed with the same kind of privilege, bitching about ennui and being misunderstood, she'd want to punch the girl in the head. What right did Lizzie Decker have to complain about anything? Her life was a guaranteed success. In four years she'd have a degree from a top ten school and go to work at her dad's company, showing up three days a week, taking off time whenever she wanted and still bringing home more money in a month than the Mexicans who did their gardening would in a year. She'd marry a polished, well-groomed poli sci major who cared about urban farming and sustainable planning, then she'd push out a couple kids. Nipped, tucked, returned to new like her mother, she'd start using summer as a verb, complain that her house was too big to get wireless in all the rooms. Except she'd do so without a hint of irony or self-reflection. Even though this future disgusted her, there didn't seem to be anything she could do about it.

"You're doing it again?"

"What?"

"Staring off into space with that that stupid look on your—" Melanie stopped, following her line of sight. "What are you looking at?"

Lizzie caught herself staring at that boy again. He was younger than the kinds of guys she usually chased, and painfully self-conscious—his face burned red anytime she glanced in his general direction.

"You gotta be kidding me," Melanie blurted. "He looks fourteen. He's not even cute."

"I think he's cute."

"He looks like that scarecrow who pitches for the Giants. Those guys you were so rude to had a cabin at Lake Tahoe."

The boy was so unsure of himself, he turned over his shoulder to see who else stood there. After dating so many players, Lizzie found his lack of game endearing.

Melanie fished in her purse and pulled out a prescription bottle, toppling a pair of pills. "Mommy's Percs." She held out one for Lizzie.

"Your mother never notices her medication is missing?"

"You kidding me? She stocks a pharmacy."

The band on stage now, Get Set Go, had been a favorite of Lizzie's since she first heard them on *Grey's Anatomy* singing a song called "I Hate Everyone." They were part of the indie sound Lizzie loved. The Shins. Stars. Tilly and the Wall. Music didn't matter to Melanie; for her, it was background noise, filler, an accompaniment to whatever else she was doing, which was how she could sit in those clubs with brain-dead electronica pumping through the PA, splintering eardrums, and not miss a beat. Lizzie hated that techno garbage. Music needs to feed the soul. Real music. Real words. Real life. This.

The boy with the shaggy black hair kept stealing glances, sweeping the bangs out of his eyes, trying to look nonchalant and coming across as anything but. It was sweet, and when the beer and the pills started hitting Lizzie right, the crowd pushing forward, bringing everyone together, the lingering fog burning off and day warming up, she let herself drift closer and closer, until she stood by his side.

Kyle had never been able to talk to girls, not even the ones up in Dormundt who hardly set your world on fire. Under normal circumstances, there was no way he'd have had the courage to talk to Lizzie, which was how she'd introduced herself. Forget how pretty she was or how much older she seemed. Any other day, he'd have dropped his head and slinked away. But this wasn't any other day. The shootout at the Skunk Train. His cousin getting run over by a truck. All that money sitting in a backpack. Maybe it was not sleeping or hanging with a gang of hoodlums, but he felt himself emboldened. Like the hero in one of his father's movies. Nothing left to lose. Why shouldn't he talk to the girl?

The music was so loud Kyle couldn't be sure she heard anything he was saying, which afforded license to spill everything. And it didn't matter because she was still laughing and touching his arm. Kyle might not have known a lot about girls, but he'd have to be an idiot not to see that she was into him. Didn't make much sense. But over that last twenty-four hours, what had?

* * *

"Movies?" Lizzie said. "Which ones?"

"A bunch of them. Some comedies. Horror." When she wrinkled her nose, Kyle added. "I'm not lying. You can see his name right there in the credits."

She squeezed his arm. "I don't think you're lying."

After trying to shout above the music, which grew louder with each act, Lizzie grabbed him by the elbow, guiding them both past his weird, grubby friends, who all did double takes before offering cockeyed grins and unsubtle thumbs-up. Hand in hand, they drove past the food venders and merch tents, to the rows of Port-o-Potties by the woods. Stepping on a stump, Lizzie jumped and caught a tree branch, pushing off the john and pulling herself up until she sat on a stout limb. She waved for Kyle to join her. The expression on his face said it all: Who is this girl?

High above the crowd, Lizzie couldn't stop thinking of Postal Service's "Such Great Heights" and how perfect everything looked from far away. Kyle sat next to her. If it wasn't so teenage crush silly, she might've kissed him. Just to see what he would do. Poor guy would probably jump out of his kicks and fall to the ground.

"...and so that's why I have to get the truck out."

The band finished and Lizzie wished she'd taken the program from Melanie to see who was up next.

"What truck?"

"The one with the money? The one I was telling you about?"

He looked like his feelings were hurt. "Sorry. It's hard to hear." Lizzie waited. "Where'd you say you were from again?"

"Dormundt. Up by Willits? Mendocino? Humboldt?"

"Why are you down here again?"

"Never mind."

"Oh, don't be like that. I want to hear about it. That's why we came up here."

"It's nothing. The city towed my truck."

"You better hurry. The county adds like two hundred dollars a day. They make it impossible unless you get it out right away. They hold auctions every weekend selling seized vehicles. It's one of the biggest revenue sources for the city."

"I've heard."

Voices called from down below.

It was a hilarious sight, Melanie standing so close to the jean-jacketed riff raff, revolted, flinching each time a crust brushed her arm.

"Those are your friends?" Lizzie asked.

"No. I met them outside the impound yard earlier and they told me about the concert. I followed them up here."

"What are you doing?" Melanie shouted through cupped hands. "I have to go...to work."

Lizzie shrugged, pantomimed she couldn't hear anything. Let her suffer a little longer.

Lizzie pulled out a pen and scribbled her number on the back of a coffee club card. "I gotta run. But call me later. I have a friend who works for the DA's office. Maybe he can do something." She felt bad saying that because she would never call her ex-boyfriend Tom and ask him for a favor. And Tom wouldn't help unless it came with strings attached.

Then she leaned over and kissed him on the cheek. Partly to give him something to brag about to his friends. Mostly to piss off Melanie. The butterflies caught her by surprise.

Climbing down the tree, Lizzie didn't know why she'd passed along her number but didn't expect him to call. She gazed up, a puzzle piece from the clay, never expecting to see the shy, awkward boy again.

"I don't know what is going on with you," Melanie said as she pulled her car away from the curb. "You begged me to come along—"

"That's not true—"

"And then you ditch me to go play K I S S I N G in the trees with that spaz."

"Kyle's a nice kid."

"Kyle?" Melanie spat out the word like it was something Gwyneth Paltrow would name her kid, a piece of fruit or a fraction.

"It was nice to talk to someone not trying to get in my pants."

"That's because he wouldn't know what to do if he got in there."

"Fuck you, Melanie. Some people care what I have to say."

"Like I *don't*? You're the one who won't tell me what's going on. You were moody as hell at breakfast, acting weird and distant at the concert—"

"My father got arrested this morning."

For once Melanie didn't have anything to say.

"Cop cars were there when I got home. Hauled him off to jail."

"And you're just telling me *now*?"

"I tried telling you! But you never shut up long enough."

"What did he do? Did he…kill someone?"

"No, he didn't kill anyone. It's not fucking *Law and Order*. They're accusing him of stealing money from his charity."

Melanie steered up Buchanan, dismissing the entire conversation with an "Oh, that's all?" wave.

"It's not nothing, Mel. It's a big deal."

"You can't steal from your own charity, Lizzie. It's his money. Probably some pissed-off employee stirring shit." She gasped. "Or maybe he's having an affair."

"You're ridiculous. My father is not having an affair. He screwed up the books and it's going to be a nightmare around the house for a long time. My mother is already doing the pious, handwringing routine. You don't know what it's like. You think everything is perfect up there. It's not."

Melanie rolled her eyes. "Oh, I know. Having everything

you've ever wanted handed to you is *so* difficult. It must be so hard being Lizzie Decker."

Lizzie didn't bother answering. But, yeah, sometimes it was.

The buzz from the pot and beer—and girl—dissipated, replaced by panicked dehydration and loneliness. Even the music, which Kyle had been digging, turned dissident, discordant, producing a massive headache. Pounding cheap beer in the sun all day wasn't helping. Neither was the ragweed they were toking. Kyle wasn't an expert when it came to marijuana blends, but he could tell the difference between threaded Humboldt goodness and shitburg schwag.

Time tugged at him. More than incurring storage costs, what if he wasn't the only one who knew about the money? What if he'd been wrong about no one seeing him? Deke warned him they'd come looking. Who? Other dealers? What if Jimmy had gotten away? Could've been pot paranoia. Or maybe Kyle was wising up, pulling his head out of his ass.

Didn't matter. Sooner or later, the cops would run a DMV check and find the truck had been towed, which would help track down the rightful owner. How long till it traced back to the shootout? He had to move. But any time Kyle pressed, Raf said he couldn't call his friend yet, before he and the others would tease Kyle, like a bunch of fifth graders, calling him pretty boy because Lizzie had talked to him and not them. Kyle knew better than to use the only comeback he had. Namely that girls like that didn't talk to puffy-faced, stinky gutter punks who hadn't showered in a month. Kyle had already grown tired of Raf and the Lost Boys and was ready to ditch them. But where would he go?

They kicked around Golden Gate Park awhile, seeking out other urchins, pestering passersby for change, a strategy that worked way more than it should have but never produced anything worthwhile. Five bucks split four ways doesn't go far.

As dusk fell, the crew moved out of the park, along Stanyan, and Kyle positioned to say goodbye. He didn't know where he was going, but he wasn't getting far with this crew. His mild infatuation with Raf's stick-it-to-the-Man attitude lasted until the cold winds blew over Twin Peaks. He'd also accepted Raf was lying about knowing a guy with money. If that were half true, Raf wouldn't look like a hobo.

Maybe he could call Ronnie, think of a suitable lie. Even Deke's ex, Kristy. Although she'd only urge him to turn himself in.

"See ya," Raf said to the others, "catch up with you tomorrow." As Kyle turned to go, he threw an arm around Kyle's neck in a playful headlock. "Not you. You're coming with me."

"I have to get going. I need to get my truck out."

"And I told you I can help. I'm going to see my friend up in Diamond Heights."

"Now?"

"Right fucking now. He'll have food and beer and shit. Besides, man, what else are you going to do? It gets cold as hell out here at night."

Raf wasn't lying about that. Kyle was already starting to shiver.

CHAPTER FIFTEEN

After showering at the truck stop, Jimmy needed three things: wheels, money, and a destination. He'd taken care of the first, hot-wiring Eric Jordan's Chevy, which sat idle behind Blood and Bones. Whenever he went on the road, Jordan parked his ride at the tattoo parlor, outside his alcoholic sister's apartment. He could be gone for weeks, his sister blacked out almost as long.

Jimmy would deal with two and three on that list at his dead friend's house.

Breaking into Deke's was a risky move. Which is why he had to wait for nightfall. Dormundt PD were morons, but even a retarded squirrel gets lucky once in a while. The cops were the least of his worries. Him and Deke had lifted a hundred pounds of weed from the Mexican mob. Those fuckers weren't asking questions, and they didn't give a damn about your side of the story. They'd slit your throat, cut off your dick, stuff it in your mouth, and call it a day.

Not like Jimmy had a choice if he wanted that backpack. There must be an address in that house somewhere, a scent to sniff, a clue to point Jimmy in the right direction. Plus, Jimmy knew all about the secret bank account in the top drawer. Deke sure as shit wasn't going to be needing it anymore.

He slouched low on the drive-by, scoped the scene. Yellow ticker tape covered the front porch but otherwise the place looked abandoned. Fuck it. If the Mexicans were waiting for him, they were waiting for him. Nothing he could do about it now. He parked beneath a Sitka eave and pulled his gun, creeping along the side of the house to the back door, which he planned on kicking in.

Except no one had even bothered to lock up. Cupboards flung open, drawers overturned, clothes strewn everywhere. Deke had been in a helluva hurry to get out of there. Jimmy cracked the shutters, peering at the tips of Mendocino mountaintops shrouded in dark fog. Water from the day's dew dripped off the gutter. He braced for the cars to come screeching around the corner, semi-automatics blazing. But they never did. Jimmy tucked his gun in his belt and got to work. Get in, get out, get moving.

He left the lights off and began rifling through closets and cubbyholes, searching old mail, letters, folders, digging in baskets, boxes, anything that might store contact info. Fucking guy didn't even have a computer, his whole life a paper trail. Nothing shredded. Right there for anyone to read. Jimmy had to be out of his mind to go into business with a guy like Deke. He went room to room. He found plenty of binders containing receipts and bills, W2s, insurance and bank statements, tax shit—what kind of pot slinger keeps meticulous documents for tax purposes? But damned if he could find a single address book.

After twenty minutes of searching, Jimmy gave up and snared a beer from the fridge. He plunked down in the frayed plaid chair and popped the top. Shit, maybe he should sit here and wait for the mutherfuckers to come and get him.

Deke's money. Jimmy hopped up and made for the bedroom. The cigar box was still there. Nine hundred and fourteen bucks. That'd work. Jimmy stuffed the wad into his jeans' pocket and went to put the cigar box down, when a thought made him stop.

Deke didn't smoke cigars.

Jimmy flipped it over.

Sentimental sonofabitch.

* * *

Following an afternoon of coffee and terrible advice, Melanie said she'd call later to figure out what they were doing with their Saturday night, despite Lizzie telling her, over and over, that there wouldn't be a Saturday night.

After the heart-to-heart with her parents, Lizzie was starting to reconsider.

Her father, out on bail since noon, sat at the table, her mother at his side, same earnest pose as this morning. Dave and Elizabeth Decker were terrific at presenting the unified front. The contrite politician caught porking his intern and the long-suffering spouse standing stoically by her man.

First and foremost, they wanted their daughter, their only child, to know she could ask anything. Nothing was off the table. There were no secrets in the Decker household. They were there to answer her questions. Except when Lizzie asked whether he did it. The simple straightforward question was met with nothing but deliberate obfuscation. Not the point. Change the subject. Next question. As if Lizzie were still a little kid who could be distracted with the promise of a bright balloon.

An hour spent bickering and badgering, sidestepping and backpedaling, Lizzie was no closer to understanding what the hell was going on.

"I don't know what you want me to say, Lizzie."

"I want you to tell me if you did it."

"It's not that simple."

"Yes, it is. Either you did. Or you didn't."

"Lizzie," her mother interrupted, "it might be hard for you to see now, but when you get older—"

"Don't play that fucking card with me."

"Don't talk to your mother like that."

"I want to talk to you, alone," Lizzie said to her dad, staring at her mother.

"We're a family." He took his wife's hand. "We have no secrets."

"I'm going to bed." Lizzie headed upstairs, knowing no one would come after her, and that if one of them started to, the other would urge to "give it time." Didn't matter who played which part. It was all a performance.

The huge house perched cliffside, an Easter Egg Victorian from a storybook. The view out the big bay windows displayed the whole city, tiny, lighted cottages dotting hill and dale, down to the bridges and marina. Kyle wondered how one man could live in something so grand, all alone. Which proved less a mystery than why he'd let someone like Raf hang around. Kyle wasn't going to ask. Besides Lizzie, Jerry was the first normal person he'd met in San Francisco. The last thing he wanted to do was offend him. Kyle was grateful to be warm and indoors, with the promise of a full belly.

Raf sat at the kitchen table, scarfing big bowls of ice cream with fresh fruit toppings—raspberries, blackberries, strawberries in little egg cartons—chugging tall glasses of cold whole milk like a son returning from private school on holiday break. Kyle felt bad for thinking Raf had been lying. So far everything he'd said had proven true. Would Jerry really help him with the money to get the truck out? Right then anything seemed possible.

"Help yourself, Kyle," Jerry said. "Whatever you want. Fridge is all yours. Just to tide you over. I have some work I need to finish up, and then we'll order take-out, if that sounds good. Thai all right?"

Raf raised his spoon, grinning, bobbing, milk dribbling down his whisker-sprouted chin.

After Jerry walked away, Kyle sat down at the table with Raf, who passed what was left of the Ben and Jerry's Coffee Toffee. Which after Raf was done gorging himself wasn't much.

"What's the deal?" Kyle asked. "How do you know this guy?"

Jerry was mid-forties, polite, good-looking, well groomed. A regular dude. Didn't make any sense.

"Is he like your cousin or uncle or something?"

"What? A guy like me can't have respectable friends?"

Gazing around the kitchen, Kyle couldn't get over how sophisticated everything was, down to the hand-painted labels on the spices, which rested snug in ornate, hand-carved racks. Kyle couldn't read that far, but he'd bet, sure as salt, they were alphabetized.

"Dude, I thought you were hungry?" Raf said, waving his spoon around like a magic wand in a dreamland castle. "Eat something."

"How long you known him?"

"Jerry? Fuck, man, three, four years."

"How'd you meet him?"

"I don't know. Same way you meet anyone, I guess."

The soup kitchen? The thrift store? Guys like Jerry didn't move in the same circles as the Rafs of the world. Then again, what did Kyle care? It beat being stuck outside in the cold San Francisco night. And he *was* hungry. He hopped up and rooted through the cupboards, which were stocked with exotic-sounding foodstuffs like lentils and kamut wheat, stamped with "organic" or "locally grown for locavores," whatever that meant. All Kyle knew, it cost a pretty penny. Kristy, Deke's ex, was into all that healthy eating and lifestyle stuff. Sometimes she'd drag Kyle to the farmer's market in Cutting. She'd spend like twelve bucks for a bag of organic tomatoes and pesticide-free strawberries.

"Jerry's a cool dude," Raf said. "He's tried to get me to move in, get off the street, but I'm not into that."

Kyle settled on a gluten-free granola bar that tasted like tree bark. "You're not into what? Having a free place to live?"

"Ain't nothing free, man. It all comes with a price."

"Yeah. It's called rent."

"Nah, dawg, I ain't talking rent. It costs more than money."

"What costs more than money?"

Raf shook his head, diving back into his bowl. "Freedom,

man. This is how it starts."

"How what starts?"

"How the system chains you down. Place to live. Car to drive. Job to shackle you. More keys for the ring, man. Handcuffs are more like it. It's all part of their plan."

"Whose plan?"

"*Their* plan. To turn you into consumer, the world into commodity. Here's what's cool. Buy our brand. Oh, you don't have the money? No problem. Here's a credit card with twenty-seven percent APR. House. Car. Mortgage. Uh-oh, interest rates rising! You're in debt to your eyeballs till the day you die, a hamster spinning the wheel. Just don't look too hard at the man behind the curtain." Raf slurped the melted cream, before bringing his bowl to the sink. "Not for me. I'll sleep outside, in the fresh air, no one telling me what to do."

"Fresh air? You live in a city."

"It's a metaphor, yo." Raf spun around, reached out, and gave Kyle's shoulder a tight squeeze. "Stick with me. I'll show you how it's done."

Kyle appreciated the offer. This house was great—the possibility of a loan to get out his truck even better—but the paternal, sage tone Raf adopted was condescending. Raf wasn't any older than Kyle, and far from a rousing success. He still stank, begged for nickels, was homeless. There were myriad roads to take. Kyle wasn't following Raf's.

"Thanks," Kyle said. "But right now all I want is to get my truck out."

Raf held up his hands, a gesture to be patient, as Jerry walked back into the kitchen.

Jerry looked down at Kyle. "Did you have something to eat?"

Kyle nodded.

"Can I get you anything to drink?"

Kyle had seen beer in the fridge but didn't want to push it, minors and alcohol and all that.

"A beer, maybe?" Jerry asked, not waiting for an answer

before opening the refrigerator and extracting two longnecks, passing Raf and Kyle one each. Kyle couldn't even pronounce the name but knew it beat the piss water from earlier. A deep amber lager, the beer went down smooth.

Raf peeled off his grimy jean jacket. "All right if I take a shower, Jer?"

"Of course." He pointed at Raf's jacket. "Why don't you throw that in the wash?"

"You know how long it took me to get it this way?" Raf cracked a grin. "But I could stand to do a load with my underwear and socks."

"You know where the laundry is." Jerry slid open a kitchen drawer and pulled out a stack of menus, sifting through until he found the one he wanted. "A friend of mine is stopping by in a little while, but why don't we put in the order now? The food will be here when you're done showering. Feel free to do the same, Kyle. There's another bathroom upstairs. Raf can show you where everything is. You know what you want?"

Kyle had never eaten Thai food before. Closest thing they had in Dormundt was Chinese and sushi, which Kyle couldn't stomach. "Something with meat?"

Jerry laughed. "I'll see what I can do."

Raf dragged Kyle along, stopping at the hall closet, stocking his arms with fluffy towels smelling of lilac and lavender. Without a word, Raf pointed up the winding mahogany staircase.

"Throw down whatever you'd like washed," Jerry called from the kitchen. "I'll leave a pair of sweats and a shirt outside the door for you to borrow till yours are dry."

In the upstairs bathroom, Kyle emptied his pockets on the sink counter and stripped down, dropping his dirty clothes outside the door.

The walk-in shower was bigger than their living room back home. He cranked the knob, fogging the glass, and stepped under the pulsating stream, closing his eyes and letting the hot water wash over him.

* * *

The thick-necked, grizzled man with the gray buzz cut and Buddy Holly glasses sliced his chicken fried steak, lit cigarette in hand. He doused the brown beef in A1 and hot sauce, then popped the top off the bottle of Rolaids and tossed back a pair.

The front bell dinged. He didn't bother to look up.

"Coffee," Banks called to the waitress, before starting down the aisle with Carter to the booth where the thick-necked man sat.

The waitress brought the pot around the other end. The two Richter detectives sat opposite the man, who flashed a terse sneer, picking a piece of gristle from his tobacco-stained teeth. She poured a steaming cup for Banks. Carter waved her off.

They waited till she'd walked away.

"What'd you find out, Ordo?"

"Ain't you forgetting something?"

Carter looked at Banks, who pulled a fat envelope from his breast pocket, sliding it across the tabletop.

The Ironside gave Carter and Banks Kyle's name. Which gave them McDermott and the dead guy, too, Deke Kelly. A missing truck. A whole lot of money. Too many unconnected threads. Ordo White was the kind of man who could tie all those loose ends together with a pretty bow. A former FBI agent with the Organized Crime Drug Enforcement Division, Ordo still had his finger on the pulse, both irregular sides of it. And he didn't mind sharing what he knew. For the right price.

Ordo peeked inside the envelope, scoffing as though insulted. "Consider this one a favor." He tucked the cash away. "You two are hotter'n' shit right now." He speared a hunk of chicken fried steak, stubbing out his cigarette on the saucer, waving the waitress over.

"Wanna slap a burger on the grill for me, honey? Extra mayo." He patted his big belly. "Worked up a helluva appetite chopping wood."

The waitress—fried hair, hooded lids, and the ragged body of a woman who'd pushed out more than her share—pointed up at the clock, an oversized novelty item with rusted forks and spoons for hands. "Kitchen's closed."

Ordo leaned forward to read the name tag on her chest, then reclined and spread his arms over the back of the booth, sports coat falling open to reveal the grip of a gun and badge. "Norine, you sure you can't open it up for one more hamburger?"

Norine returned a pained grin. "I'll see what I can do."

Ordo watched her walk down the aisle.

"Your boys Deke Kelly and Jimmy McDermott were re-upping in Humboldt yesterday afternoon," he said. "Supplier named Bodhi. Social services found the bodies when they retrieved the kids."

"Do I even want to ask?"

"Execution style. Along with his two wives."

"Let me guess," Carter said. "Anonymous call?"

"Just tell us," Banks said. "How bad?"

"You boys might want to get some more coffee."

"Never touch the stuff," said Carter.

"You might want to start. 'Cause you ain't sleeping. IA's got a hard-on for you two."

"IA's always up our asses. What else is new?"

"IA is the least of your worries," said Ordo. "The skunk belonged to the Mexicans."

"Doesn't it all?"

"No. It *belonged* to the Mexicans. Kelly and McDermott stole it from them."

"Morsman fucked us," Banks said to Carter.

"We'll deal with him later." Carter turned to Ordo. "What happened?"

"Petty crook named Lester Doyle and his outfit were planning on pinching it from Bodhi after the transfer. There's been a shortage up here of late." He winked. "But you boys wouldn't know anything about that, would you?" Ordo licked his fingers clean of grease. "Something went wrong."

"Like what?"

"I don't know. But McDermott and Kelly got to it first."

Norine brought Ordo's burger. He picked up the bun, which was devoid of extra mayo. In fact devoid of it all together. Before he could protest, Norine held up a hand. "All out."

Ordo grimaced.

"I don't suppose the Mexicans will take a refund?"

"You know better than that. You break it, you bought it. They want their cash. And that's not all. One of Doyle's boys offed a member of the cartel, and the Mexicans ain't looking to play nice. Found Lester Doyle's body last night. Along with his buddies, Paul Craven and Cormack McKay, dicks stuffed in their mouth. Y'know it ain't about the money with those mutherfuckers."

"Anything else?" asked Carter.

"Only that a detective up in Cutting has been pulling every file they can find on you two, talking to IA. And IA is being extra helpful, if you know what I mean." He studied them. "You do something to piss Cutting off? This seems personal."

Carter and Banks said nothing.

"Ain't none of my business." Ordo chomped half the burger in one bite, talking while he chewed. "We go way back. I like you boys. Can I give you some advice? Whatever you've stashed from all your scams and schemes over the years, take it. Run. Don't walk. Get the fuck out of Dodge. This is not going to end well."

"We need to get the money back," Banks said without hesitation.

Ordo swallowed his meat. "What about you, Ray?"

"We're getting the money back."

Ordo shook his head, reclined, opened his arms, and twiddled his fat fingers. "Give me the number."

Carter handed him a scrap of paper with the license plate's info.

"I'll check the toll cameras. Maybe you'll get lucky and someone will cite the kid for underage driving, stick him somewhere safe until you can talk to him." Ordo shoved the rest of the burger down his gullet. "I'll pull a few strings. Then we're going to call it a day. No offense, but talking to you two right now is career suicide."

CHAPTER SIXTEEN

Kyle heard scuffling outside the bathroom door. He shut off the water, his hands shriveled and pink as newborn field mice.

"Hello?" He scrubbed his long hair dry and wrapped the towel around his skinny waist. "Anyone there?"

A bright full moon shone through the high skylight, splashing down on the cool tile.

Kyle tiptoed to the door and cracked it open. A pair of sweats and a polo shirt rested on the floor, folded like a department store display.

"Yo," Raf called, popping his head above the top step, looking freshly scrubbed and clean-shaven. You could almost see what he was like before he took on this life. "Food's here, dawg. Better hurry up and get dressed before there ain't no spring rolls left."

Kyle slipped one foot in the sweats as he hopped along the carpet runner, pulling the peach polo, a size too big, over his wet body. The exotic scents of warm spices you don't find at Taco Bell or Geiger's Market wafted up the well, along with waves of robust laughter.

"Thought you'd drowned in there," Jerry said.

"No shit, man," added Raf, who, like Kyle, now modeled threads better suited for the country club than the mean streets. "You were in there like forty minutes."

"Sorry. Didn't realize I'd taken so long."

"No worries," said Jerry, as another man emerged from the

corridor. "This is my friend, Mike. Mike, Kyle. Kyle, Mike."
He looked like Jerry. Of course everyone over the age of thirty
looked the same to Kyle.

"Nice to meet you," Mike said, reaching for a handshake.

"Dig in, boys. Want anything to drink? Another beer?"

"Got anything stronger?" Raf asked.

Jerry waggled a tsk-tsk finger, then turned to Mike, who
smirked, as if to say boys will be boys. "Want to grab the
Balvenie 21 out of the cabinet?"

"The good stuff."

"Why not? We're celebrating."

Kyle furrowed his brow. "What are you celebrating?"

Jerry and Mike exchanged a look, then Jerry said, "Mike and
I work together. Landed a new client. Boring stuff for boys your
age. But very exciting for old men like us."

Mike clinked some ice from the freezer and poured four tall
glasses of whiskey.

Kyle had thought maybe Jerry didn't know how old he was,
which was why he was so easy going with the booze. But he
called him a boy, and even on his best day, in the most flatter-
ing light, Kyle couldn't pass for more than eighteen, so maybe
Jerry didn't care. So why should he?

Jerry began dishing the takeout, steaming piles of rainbow-
colored entries and side dishes, appetizers with fragrant aromas,
fried beef with chilies and crisp greens, pork on soft beds of
lettuce, minty and peppery, garlic and basil too, warm mounds of
rice, coconut soups, breaded chickens bathed in deep red bases.

Everyone was laughing, Jerry and Mike quick with clever
quips. Kyle couldn't keep up until the conversation steered to
movies.

"My father's a director," he said.

"Like in Hollywood?"

Kyle dunked a spring roll in sticky sweet sauce. "Yup. A
bunch of movies."

"Anything we'd know?"

"He did one about OJ Simpson, thrillers, mysteries, TV shows. The most famous one he did was one of the *Hellraisers*."

"Don't know it," Jerry said.

"Yeah you do," said Raf. "Considered, like, the worst movie of all time."

Kyle ignored Raf's dig.

"I love *all* the *Hellraisers*," Mike said, before turning to Kyle. "What's your dad's name?"

"Alan. Smith. He spells it different though. That's his stage name, the one he uses for business."

Mike and Jerry again glanced at each other, eyebrows raised. Disbelief? Mocking? Didn't matter. People never believed Kyle when he told them about his father.

"When was the last time you saw your dad?" Raf chided.

"He's pretty busy."

"You don't live with him then I take it?" Jerry said.

"No. I live...with my cousin, Deke."

"In the city?"

"No, up north, like by Richter. Small town." Kyle didn't feel like going into it more than that.

"Long way from home," Mike said.

Kyle stared at Raf. "I'm on my way to visit my dad right now, in fact."

"Don't you have school?"

"We're on break."

Raf grumbled.

"I think it's terrific you're going to visit your dad," Mike said. "A boy your age needs a father figure, someone to usher him into manhood. Maybe he'll get to show you around town. I lived in L.A. for a while. Old Hollywood. Many of the settings they used for the classics are still there, Untouched, wonderful." Mike picked up the scotch. "Anyone need a refill?"

Raf chugged the rest of his drink and raised the glass. Kyle hadn't taken more than a couple sips and already his head felt woozy. He didn't want to say anything since Mike and Jerry had made such a big deal over how expensive it was, but Kyle thought the liquor tasted like underarm sweat.

Jerry began collecting plates, and Raf started bragging about his band, which was hysterical since the guy was homeless and couldn't possibly own an instrument.

"Like the Dead Boys," Raf said. "But harder. Less melodic. We got a bunch a killer gigs lined up. Then we go into the studio. Cut an album. Bunch a labels are already interested."

Kyle knew what he was doing. He had a famous dad in Hollywood, so Raf had to one-up him.

After Jerry finished stacking the washer, he said he was going into his office and asked Raf to join him, something about a new stereo system he wanted him to check out. Raf grabbed the bottle, their footsteps echoing down cavernous halls.

"Have you seen Jerry's movie collection?" Mike asked.

"No. This is the first time I've been here. In fact I just met Raf today."

"Figured. You don't seem like the kind of guy who'd hang out with Raf." And he winked to let Kyle know he also thought Raf was a tool. This Mike was pretty cool. "Check it out. If you're into movies, I think you'll appreciate his library." Mike started toward the living room. "We'll see if we can find any your father directed."

The living room was like a movie theater with a TV almost as big as a Cineplex screen, towering pair of speakers on each side. And Mike wasn't kidding. Jerry housed a massive collection. He had DVDs stacked in tall, wide cases, floor to ceiling, like most people do with books. He had plenty of those as well.

Mike came and stood beside him, bringing his drink. "Forgot something."

Kyle's face screwed up.

"Not much of a scotch man, eh?" Mike leaned in. "Want to know a secret? Me neither. More of a beer guy." He made for the kitchen. "I'm going to grab one. You?"

"Sure."

Mike said something else but Kyle couldn't hear what because the rooms in Jerry's house, with their open air ceilings and exposed cedar beams, spread out wider than a country barn.

Kyle stood at the window staring at city lights that shone down to the beach and shipyards, the towering cranes and freighters. Kyle wouldn't mind being on one of those big boats right now, shipping off to somewhere far from here, a new country, a new life.

"…the first thing I got drunk on. Haven't been a fan since."

"Huh?"

Mike passed Kyle the beer. "Scotch. You didn't hear a word I said, did you?"

"Sorry. This house is so big."

"Helluva view though." Mike stood next to Kyle, pointing out to the sea. "When I was a kid, I used to think the seafaring life was so romantic. Don't laugh, but I wanted to sail the world. Even joined the Navy. For a while."

Kyle peered up at him, but Mike waved a hand. "Boring story. You don't want to hear about that."

"What do you do now?"

"You mean for work?" Mike again brushed him off. He retreated to the couch, patting a seat for Kyle to join him. "I'd rather hear about you. I'm getting the sense that something is happening with you, more than you're letting on."

Kyle sat and shrugged.

"I thought so. Listen, Kyle, I know you don't know me. I'm just some strange guy you met in some strange man's house."

"I don't think you're strange."

Mike laughed. "Okay. A stranger. But I was your age once. I know that seems hard to believe. This might sound pedantic, but I remember how hard an age that was. What are you? Eighteen?"

"Sixteen."

"Sixteen." Mike blew out a breath. "Almost seventeen?"

Kyle nodded. He didn't see any point correcting him that it

was the other way around, fifteen almost sixteen.

"The thing is, Kyle. I'm forty-two now." He pulled back. "Do I look it?"

Kyle didn't answer right away.

"I know. I do." Mike ran his hands through his hair. "At least I still got this."

Kyle would've told him he looked good for his age—and he did, like he worked out, watched what he ate; he didn't look like the forty-year-olds up in Dormundt, with their trucker's caps, bushy beards, and bulging guts—but guys don't tell other guys stuff like that.

"I remember how alienated I felt at your age. Lonely. It can be real lonely, and you feel like you can't tell anyone anything. Sure as hell can't trust them. And if you get in a jam, something bad happens, forget asking for help." Mike studied him. "I'm sensing you're in some kind of trouble, a young man shoulder-ing a tremendous burden. I know we just met but I want you to know I'm a good listener, Kyle. And I don't judge. If you want to try me out. I can be a good friend to you."

Kyle felt the incredible urge to purge, spill everything. The stolen marijuana. The money. Watching his cousin die. Even Lizzie. Not because he liked this guy, or even trusted him, but because aside from Lizzie he was the first person down here who'd shown any real interest in his life.

"What are you thinking right now?" Mike asked. "Your whole body tensed up. I can see it in your face, shoulders stiff as stone. Here, turn around." Mike gently spun him. "I learned this from my massage therapist. You'd be amazed at how much stress our bodies carry. People think it's all in your head, the pain and anguish, but it's all connected. Western medicine wants us to pop a pill to make the hurt go away. But you want to heal the soul and mind, you need to heal the body as well."

Mike pressed his thumbs hard into Kyle's upper spine, causing him to flinch. "I know. Trust me. Try and relax. Close your eyes. Think of somewhere warm, safe. Maybe a favorite childhood memory? Was there a place you liked to go when you were little? With your parents perhaps? A special spot in the woods?"

Something about "a spot in the woods" took Kyle to a place he hadn't visited in a long time. Kyle's memory of his mother was fleeting, came in fits and bursts, random patterns of light, and when he thought of her, it was always in black-and-white, never color. Suddenly he was young again, small, just walking. He shouldn't have been able to go back that far, he knew conscious memories didn't start forming until age four or five, but in this memory he was much younger than that, like two, and it would've had to have been around then because his mom died when he was five, and by that point she had been long bedridden. He recalled walking side by side, the imagery colorful and crisp, vibrant, vivid, sun cresting high in the summer sky. She held his hand, pointing out birds in a tree. Sunlight refracted through leaves, and he felt so safe having his mother with him. It was a love permanent and unwavering, like she would never leave him, and it was such a good, warm, safe feeling, one he hadn't felt in such a long time, that he wanted to cry. Then he felt the hand kneading his crotch.

He jumped up. "What the hell?!"

Mike showed his hands, a flirty expression on his face, as if he'd been caught sneaking an extra piece of someone else's birthday cake. Now it all made sense, and Kyle felt like a moron for not figuring it out sooner. Holy shit he was clueless.

"What the hell?" Kyle repeated, swatting at his crotch like he'd stumbled into an attic full of cobwebs and the lingering memory still gave him the heebie jebbies.

"Relax, Kyle. Sit down. I misunderstood."

"Misunderstood what?"

"I was trying to give you a massage—"

"Yeah, massage my dick. Fucking pervert."

"Whoa. Calm down. Don't talk like that."

"I'm sorry," Kyle said, feigning remorse. "I meant, fucking pedophile!"

Jerry and Raf rushed into the room, Jerry buttoning up his pants, Raf without a shirt.

"What's going on? Everything okay?"

"No," Kyle said. "Everything is not *okay*. He tried to stick his hand down my pants!"

Jerry blew out a gust. "Okay. Let's relax. Everyone have a seat. Kyle, I'm sure it's a misunderstanding."

"Why's everyone keep saying that? There's nothing to misunderstand!" Kyle's head panned from Jerry to Mike to Raf, who refused to look at him as if Kyle was the one out of line. "What is wrong with you people?"

"I'm sorry," Mike said, standing up and reaching for Kyle's shoulder to give a good-natured pat.

He jerked away. "Screw this. I'm outta here."

"Hold on. It's late and you—"

But Kyle was already out the door. From the corner of his eye, he could see Jerry flapping for Mike to let him go. Didn't matter. No way Kyle was staying in that house a second longer.

He stomped down the front steps to the sidewalk, the frigid winds from the bay stopping him cold in his tracks. Raf came bounding down after him.

"What's your problem, man?"

Kyle spun around. "What's *my* problem? You bring me to a house so a couple old perverts can molest us—and you're asking what *my* problem is?"

"I fucking did you a favor. Wandering around like a little baby because you lost your car. I let you hang around with my friends, got you food, cleaned you up, and this is how you repay me? Insult the two guys who can actually *help* you?"

"Help me? How? By sticking their dicks in my mouth?"

"That's the way it works. Asshole. I don't know how you do up in hillbilly country, but down here you get for what you give."

Kyle shook his head. He felt sorry for Raf. "How can you let them do that to you?"

"Fuck you." Raf shoved Kyle against the brick wall. "You

live in a fantasy world. With your make-believe, rich, famous daddy. You're pathetic."

"He's not make-believe."

"Yeah? Then why don't you call him? Here's some money." Raf fisted coins from his pocket and flung them at Kyle, who covered up as nickels and dimes pinged his face and splashed on the sidewalk. "Go on. Pick them up. Call Daddy." Raf leaned his puffy, mean face in, pouting his lower lip. "Oh, that's right. You don't have his number. You don't even know where he lives."

Kyle, who had felt so strong and righteous storming out, could feel the tears building. Please don't let him cry now.

"That's because he doesn't exist." Raf turned to leave.

"Have fun sucking cock—"

The right landed flush on his nose, which cracked and filled with blood. The blow must've knocked him for a second because next thing Kyle knew he was lying on his back, alone, smearing blood onto the back of his hand, gazing up at a million tiny stars, wishing he could fly away to one of them and never come back.

CHAPTER SEVENTEEN

"This is turning into a weekend ritual with us," Jacobs joked.

Nomura wasn't laughing. In the six months they'd worked together, she hadn't smiled once. How did he end up with a partner so joyless?

She steadied her steps down the slick, moss-covered stones to the river's edge and the bloated blue body that lay on the shore, the early morning mist hovering ghostly above the waters.

"Say hello to Chip Morsman." Jacobs sipped his coffee and made a bitter face. The thing he missed most about L.A.? A decent cup of joe. "What do you think?"

Nomura snapped on the latex gloves and squatted next to the corpse, pointing at the bruises around his neck. "Asphyxiated. Ligature marks. Telephone cord maybe."

"Was staying at the Sunshine Motel off the Lakeview." He dumped the rest of his swill in the tall reeds. "Neighbors reported seeing an undercover cop car late last night hauling him off. Nothing in the system. I guess your far-fetched theory about rogue police officers wasn't so far-fetched."

"You pegging Banks and Carter for this?"

Jacobs upturned his palms. "Hey, it was *your* theory. I'm saying this lends credibility to it. Soon as we start poking around looking for Morsman, he ends up face down in the Eel River? Interesting timing, no?"

Nomura stood back up on the bank as medical personnel and forensics descended through the woods with stretcher and sheet.

"Too bad you didn't find him yesterday," she said.

"Wasn't for lack of effort. Spent the whole day searching. Scoped out every motel and skid row dump along that wretched road. Drug dens. Shooting galleries. Even the shelter in Northspur. I looked everywhere."

"Except the Sunshine."

"Except the Sunshine."

"What do we do now?"

"Treat Carter and Banks like suspects. Cops or not. We've got a pair of dangerous animals in a dirty hole they dug, willing to do anything to crawl out. Way I'm playing this, Carter and Banks set up the shady deal at the Skunk Train, everything went to hell, and now they are covering their tracks."

"Captain Sturgis in Richter says money is missing from evidence."

"I'd wager a year's pay it's the same cash Carter and Banks used to stage the buy."

"What about eyewitness reports of a third man?"

"Obviously Morsman."

Nomura grimaced. "That would make this tidy."

"Once we find the drugs and money, it will." Jacobs turned to her. "Any leads on Gill?"

"We got one troubled kid. Kyle Gill hasn't been to school in weeks. Got a hold of the school shrink. Wasn't easy to do on a weekend. You know how far they bus those kids from Dormundt?"

"Somewhere between a Coal Miner's Daughter and Little House on the Prairie?"

"Huh?"

"Never mind. Bad joke. What'd the shrink tell you?"

"Sounded relieved he stopped going. Picture she painted had him about an hour from donning a trench coat and mowing down his graduating class."

"You're not buying it?"

"I think schools respond to teen angst with a one-size-fits-all approach. But I can't say for sure. Never met the boy."

"Any idea where he'd be right now?"

"He has an estranged father down in your old stomping grounds."

"L.A.?"

"Works in the movies. At least that's the story."

"You're not buying that either?"

"I don't know. What's your interest in this boy? Shouldn't our priority be finding James McDermott?"

"It is. But the same witnesses who saw McDermott fleeing through the forest put Kyle Gill at the Skunk Train. Someone took McDermott's truck. Now Kyle is missing."

"He's just a kid."

"And a very disturbed one, from the sounds of it. Any friends?"

"One." Nomura pulled a slip of paper from her pocket. "Ronnie Salk. Lives up on The Arlington."

"Nice neighborhood. Let's pay Ronnie a visit." Jacobs started up the embankment, stopped and turned over his shoulder. "Well, come on," he said, smiling. "But first we're stopping for a real cup of coffee somewhere."

Kyle woke on the damp ground beneath a bush in Golden Gate Park, teeth chattering, nothing but a muddy polo and crummy pair of sweats carrying him through the frigid San Francisco night.

After his fight with Raf, Kyle hadn't staggered two blocks before realizing the real damage of that cold cock: he'd left everything he owned on the bathroom counter upstairs. His wallet. The PG&E bill with his uncle's address. The pocket change that would've at least afforded a goddamn donut. Not to mention, the phone number of the only person he knew in the city, who also happened to be the prettiest girl he'd ever met: Lizzie.

So he'd set off through the cold midnight fog like a hobo

kicked off a freighter, lost, alone, trapped in a city that didn't want him. He sure as hell wasn't going back to that house. He wandered up to the park and found some bushes, pulled his arms inside his shirt, curled into bed hugging himself, and drifted off to the most uncomfortable night of sleep in his life.

The sun hadn't been up long and already the festivalgoers were streaming back in the park, hundreds of tapered pants and V-neck sweaters passing by, not even glancing down at Kyle, like he was another bum.

Kyle stood and stretched, wiping the exhaustion from his eyes. Then he rubbed his arms trying to get circulation flowing again, watching his breath crystalize.

"Why didn't you pick up your phone last night?" Melanie snapped.

Lizzie was asking herself why she'd picked up this time.

She had left the house before her parents would know she was gone, driving in circles, playing Broken Social Scene, trying not to think. Spent an hour and a half drinking cooling coffee and pawing a raspberry scone at Happy Beans on Valencia, watching the murk and drizzle through the window, before ducking into Community Thrift next door, where she sifted through an uninspiring rack.

"I don't know why I'm up at this hour," Melanie said.

"It's almost eleven o'clock." Lizzie perused the next aisle, killing time. Though what she was waiting for, she couldn't say. All she knew was she wanted to stay away from home. When Melanie didn't respond, Lizzie knew enough to play along. "Fine. Why *are* you up so early?"

"Because when I couldn't get ahold of you. I stayed in and fell asleep at eight-thirty like a fucking grandpa."

Lizzie laughed. "You slept away your Saturday night?"

"Tell me about it."

The clerk spun the Smiths, and Morrissey was pleading to

please, please, please let him get what he wanted this time. She empathized. Outside the windows, cars raced along slick city streets blanketed in heavy fog. Cradling the phone, Lizzie inspected a hideous blue sailor's jacket missing a button.

"Anyway," Melanie said, "I wanted to call to say I'm sorry."

"About what?"

"Being a shitty friend. I didn't know what was going on with your dad, and I was making it worse for you."

Lizzie draped the clothes she didn't want back over the rack, and exited the store, ducking into the swirling wind and cold.

"What are you doing now?" Melanie said. "I have all afternoon before work. Want to grab brunch? I can call Jax and—"

"I'm thinking of going back up to the park."

"Why? No good bands go on till later."

Lizzie unlocked her car.

"Wait. You're not going back to see that weird kid, are you?"

"He's not weird."

Lizzie hadn't realized she'd decided to return to the park and look for Kyle until Melanie said it, which was stupid anyway, given how many people would be at the concert. No guarantee he'd even be there. Had she really developed a crush after a ten-minute conversation in a tree? At least she knew what she'd been waiting for. Jesus, her head was a mess. Obviously, he wasn't interested, or he would've called. Or maybe he was as shy as he seemed. Either way, she wouldn't mind catching Death Cab.

"Did he call?"

"No." Lizzie sat in the idling car, wipers swishing mist, heat blasting. "I know. I'm being stupid."

"Maybe he lost your number?"

"You think so?"

"It's possible. Are you there now?"

"Driving up."

"Want some company?"

* * *

Carter sat on the lumpy bed inside the roadside motel, well south of Dormundt, a tiny television straining for reception through the tall, clustered pines, waiting for the phone to ring.

Cops up here did it all the time. That's why half of them transferred to Humboldt County, the loss in salary compensated by the free drug money. Everyone dealt. Every cop skimmed off the top. It was an unspoken agreement. Why did they have to be the ones to get sacked?

"We pin it on Doyle," Banks said, clicking off the TV. "It's not like he's talking. Or Morsman. Who'd believe that junkie piece of shit?"

Carter didn't say anything.

"Or we could tell the truth."

Carter cast an agitated sideways glance.

"Someone's gotta take the fall."

"My guess is the two guys who've had IA up their asses for the last six months. It doesn't make a difference what *we* say. There's good cops. And bad cops. Guys like Jacobs are the good guys. And, sorry, brother, we're the other ones. He's in charge of the investigation, and he'll be coming hard. There are no friends, no partners in crime. There are heroes and patsies. This is all getting pinned on us." Carter lit a cigarette.

"Could've brought a suitcase filled with shredded newspaper to the Skunk Train. Those dipshits wouldn't have known the difference."

"Doesn't matter now, does it?"

"What then? We run? Because even if we bring that cash back, we're finished in Richter. We're looking at time."

"Don't you think I know that?"

"If half of what Ordo said is true…"

"Doesn't matter. That hundred grand is a bargaining chip. At the very least, it's a nice severance package. What'd your guy at highway patrol say?"

"Takes a while to go through toll road footage." Banks waited. "The kid's, what, fifteen?"

"Your point?"

"Maybe Ordo's right and we got lucky and a cop pulled him over? Check the impound yards."

"You know how long that'd take? We don't have the pull Ordo does."

"So we wait for him."

"I'm not sure Ordo is sticking his neck out anymore. You heard him. We're too damn hot. We can wipe them all out. Morsman. Jacobs. Even the kid. It's still all coming back on us. Face it, no one is coming to our rescue."

The telephone rang.

CHAPTER EIGHTEEN

Kendra Johnson didn't know who was buzzing her bell at this hour, but it was one of two possibilities. Either some joker looking to get high (which Kendra had already taken care of last night, enjoying a deep, opiate-induced slumber, so whoever it was could fuck off), or her son Jay Jay was bringing Alec back because some new emergency had come up. And that wasn't happening. Kendra loved her grandson, but she'd raised four of her own and if Jay Jay could handle getting that crazy bitch pregnant, he could handle the repercussions. Jay Jay had made a big deal out of wanting to be a better father, how he could take care of his own son without the help of social services or his mama bailing him out; the mutherfucker was going to take his weekends, like it or not. No shortcuts. No take backs.

The ringing was relentless, nonstop, killing her high and pissing her off. When no one answered after she called down, just kept ringing, she buzzed them in. Whoever was down there was about to learn why you don't wake up Kendra Johnson first thing Sunday morning.

Ready to tear someone a new asshole, Kendra jerked back the door and had a change of heart.

The man wasn't that big, didn't look especially aggressive. White boy. Late-twenties. Dirty, short reddish-blond hair. Farm boy-looking mutherfucker. Kendra outweighed him by a good twenty. It was the eyes. Something screwy in them. Not rapist or dope fiend screwy. More the look of a man who had something he wanted and thought you could give it to him. And if you did, he might be on his way. But if you couldn't? Just as liable to break your neck and throw you down a flight of stairs, make himself a sandwich on the way out.

Kendra backed away from the door and allowed the man inside. He smiled, or maybe it was more a snarl; she couldn't tell the difference. As he passed, she knew if he'd had a cowboy hat, he would've tipped that too.

"Been out there all night," he said. "Ringing that bell. Must've been some good shit."

"What do you want?"

"I'm looking for my brother."

Kendra relaxed a bit. That sweet, nervous boy from yesterday. Almost had forgotten about him. He'd shown up as Jay Jay was collecting Alec to bring him down to San Bruno for visiting hours.

"He borrowed my truck without my permission. I need it back."

"Where he borrow it from?"

"Our house."

"Where's your house?"

"Up north."

There was that look again.

"He come by here or not?"

Kendra bent down and started to clean up, although she wasn't sure why. Just to be doing something—a clean apartment had never been her thing. She didn't care about that boy from yesterday, but there was something helpless about him, maybe it was the mother in her that wanted to protect. The long, stringy hair. Him trying to act tough, when everyone could see he was a lost puppy trying to find his—what did he say? Uncle? Father? That deadbeat fuck Joe who'd lived here before her. But this guy...Forget the different hair color or the crooked nose that had been broken in too many bar fights. Kendra had four kids, four different daddies, and ain't none of them looked alike. But you could tell they were related just the same. Kendra didn't know this guy's story, but she was sure of one thing: he wasn't that boy's brother.

"What you say your name was?" she asked, continuing to chuck random items in a bucket.

"I didn't." The man grabbed a lighter off a CD floured with white dust. He didn't ask if he could smoke, just slid a cigarette out the pack, bringing it to his lips.

"I don't know who told you what," Kendra said, "but nobody's been by here."

The man picked up a stack of bills, leafing through them. He held one up. "Joe Kelly. You don't look like a Joe."

"Former tenant, used to live here before me."

"How long?"

"What?"

"How long ago did he live here?" He drew each word out.

"Four, five years. I don't remember."

"And you keep his mail because, what? You miss him?"

Kendra decided she'd misread this guy. Maybe he was that kid's brother. But Kendra Johnson would be damned if she'd let some backwoods clown walk into *her* home and push her around. She'd brought up four kids in the Tenderloin, kept a hundred-dollar-a-day habit going, and dealt with some of the nastiest mutherfuckers this city had to offer. It also helped that Jay Jay kept his Glock in the kitchen.

Kendra walked back there like she was going to empty the trash, then opened the cupboard, reaching for the Jumbo Folgers. She caught his reflection in the tin.

He grabbed her by the neck, squeezing so hard she started to squeal, which made him clutch harder, crushing her windpipe, and she knew not to make any more noise.

"Listen, lady," the man said, calm as if asking to borrow a cup of milk from a neighbor. "I want to know where my brother is, okay?"

Kendra had sunk to one knee, throat burning as she tried

twisting for the relief he wouldn't grant. She felt the cold steel pressing into her temple.

"I ain't playing, hon. Where's Joe Kelly living these days? Don't tell me you don't know."

"L.A., I think."

He pinched her neck harder.

"Collection agency called once. Said SoCal."

"You tell Kyle that? He taking my truck to find his uncle in Los Angeles?"

"Towed...the...truck."

"Don't fucking lie to me, bitch."

"I'm not...lying. That boy come here, they towed the truck he was driving. I gave him some utility bills, he walked out and they was towing the truck. You...can call the impound yard and...check...it out."

He let her go, and Kendra slumped to the floor.

"I will. And if you're lying to me? I'll come back and put a bullet in your stupid junkie head."

Bumming a cigarette was hard in this town. Half the people scowled like you'd asked to set their lungs on fire, which was funny, the air so saturated with pot, and the rest acted like you wanted to borrow a hundred bucks. What was the big deal? It was a lousy goddamn cigarette.

Took a while but Kyle managed to score one, and it might've been the best smoke he ever had. Golden Gate Park crawled with couples and cute girls setting up picnic blankets with snacks and sandwiches. Kyle wished he'd taken more advantage of the free food last night. His stomach rumbled.

He didn't know where he was going, the grounds so vast, but he soon found himself standing beneath the same tree he'd climbed yesterday.

This was a nightmare. No money. Except the fortune sitting in the truck, waiting to get discovered by the cops, who had to be on his trail by now. And if the cops didn't get him first, there was always the bikers or whoever the stuff belonged to. And what was he doing? Standing beneath some tree, hoping a girl he barely knew would appear, because he'd been too dumb to hold onto the one way he had to get ahold of her in a city of millions. He couldn't beat himself up anymore if he were punching his own stupid face.

Kyle felt a tug on his sleeve.

It made Melanie sick to listen to. The way they carried on, you would've thought they met at summer camp, like, back in 1999, and had run into each other by chance in Paris ten years later. Ridiculous. Lizzie met this freak show yesterday and was glomming on to him now because her home life was such a disaster. Which did make Melanie feel a little bad for her. But not *too* bad. Lizzie had always had everything handed to her. Gorgeous, rich, as popular as she wanted to be. As comfortable with the cheerleaders as she was the debate team. Lizzie chose to hang around with the rejects and castoffs because it made her feel superior. If Melanie had her life, she sure as hell wouldn't be wasting it on losers like this Kyle. But Melanie didn't have her life. No schools were lining up to pay her way to college. Guys didn't fight over her. Melanie had to work at a chintzy consignment shop, squirreling away money if she wanted to go to college. Even though she knew she'd end up at State.

"I would've called," Kyle said trying not to smile too much. "But I...lost your number. Not on purpose. I left it behind at this house I couldn't go back to."

"I'm here now. Did you ever get your truck out?"

Kyle shook his head.

"And you can't call your parents?" Lizzie asked.

"Don't have any."

Melanie scoffed. "I thought you told Lizzie your dad's, like, a famous movie director."

"He *is* a director. But I can't call him about something like this. I don't need his money. I *have* money."

"Then why don't you use it to get your truck out?" Melanie rolled her eyes at Lizzie.

"That's the problem. My money is in the truck, and the impound guy won't let me get it out to pay them."

"That's messed up," Lizzie said.

"I know, right? I tried explaining a hundred times."

"I'll put it on my credit card. And you can pay me back."

"What?" Melanie blurted.

"Your money's in the truck, right?"

"Yeah."

"No problem then."

"Can I talk to you a second?"

"Be right back." Lizzie tried to keep the smile over her shoulder as Melanie whisked them out of earshot behind a falafel vendor.

"Are you out of your fucking mind? If that truck's been in there two days, that's, like, a thousand bucks."

"So? He'll pay me right back."

Melanie pointed at Kyle. He'd looked goofy yesterday in his Farmer Brown get-up; he looked even stranger today, sporting the road uniform for a gay volleyball team. "And you believe him? He looks like he slept outside last night. People with money don't sleep in the park."

"He explained where his money is."

"He also said his father is a famous Hollywood director. He's obviously full of shit. If you want to give someone a thousand dollars, I'll be happy to take it!"

"Calm down, Mel. It's not your money. It's mine. And I can loan it to whoever I choose." Lizzie waved Kyle over. "You don't have to come."

"Oh, I'm coming."

Melanie wasn't letting some hillbilly scam her best friend.

CHAPTER NINETEEN

When they got to AutoReturn, Lizzie ached to prove Melanie wrong. Melanie liked to act like such a tough, big city chick, but that's all it was: an act. Within her own circle, she could push people around, which she'd been doing to Lizzie for years. Lizzie hated admitting, if even to herself, how little she'd miss her when she went to Occidental.

True, Melanie hadn't gotten the breaks Lizzie had, but how was that Lizzie's fault? Other people being happier than Melanie, which was damn near everyone, pissed her off. She manipulated every circumstance in her favor, from splitting bills at restaurants to going in on gas, whatever she had to do to level a make-believe playing field. Melanie couldn't believe anyone else was honest and forthright. In her world, trust equated to stupidity.

Except when they stepped inside the impound office, the situation became clear. Something wasn't right.

Forget the depressing-as-shit atmosphere, the phony empathetic posters plastered on the wall—they had pictures of people crying, tearing their hair out, with reassurances that the city understood how frustrating it must be to lose your car—when *they* were the ones who'd taken it. Only in San Francisco would they try to turn having your car towed into a teachable moment. Even on a Sunday, the place drew a crowd, hungover hipsters paying the price for trying to squeeze in and make one last Guerrero Street bar before closing time.

When one of the windows opened, Lizzie, in a show of faith,

and perhaps to show up Melanie, handed over her credit card to the man behind the glass. Lizzie even chastised the man for being rude to her friend yesterday, but Kyle explained it was a different guy. Still the man apologized and said he'd be happy to help. Then he asked for Kyle's license, which was when things began turning weird. Kyle didn't have one.

The other three looked at each other.

The man stared.

"I lost my wallet."

"Do you have a license number?"

Kyle didn't say anything.

"How old are you, son?" the man asked.

"He's sixteen," Lizzie said.

"I'm fifteen."

Melanie snickered.

"I'll be sixteen soon."

"So you don't *have* a license?" the man said.

"Technically? No."

"What do you mean 'technically'? Either you have one or you don't."

"Then I don't. I have a learner's permit. I'm not from here." Kyle waited. "I live up north. Like by Willits."

"Which means you can't drive on the highway to get down here," the man said. "Let's see the permit."

"Told you. I lost my wallet."

The man behind the counter looked at Lizzie, who could only shrug. "Okay, kid," he said. "Let's try this another way. What's your last name?"

Kyle spelled it out and the man typed it in.

Lizzie didn't like where this was going.

"No truck under that name, sorry. You sure it was towed here?"

Kyle nodded.

"It wasn't towed in Daly City or Fremont or somewhere else? Because this is just for cars towed within SF city limits."

"It was towed here," Kyle said, face turning red.

"Was this your mom's car? Dad's?"

Kyle shook his head no, as the customers behind them began to shuffle and moan.

"I don't know what to tell you," the man said, pointing past his shoulder. "I've got to take care of—"

"The thing is," Kyle said, leaning in and whispering, like maybe Lizzie wouldn't be able to hear, even though she stood about a foot away, "it's not *my* truck."

"Whose truck is it?"

"Just this...guy," Kyle said.

"My advice is to call your friend and have him come down here, because I can't give you a truck that doesn't belong to you."

"I can't call him. He's not a friend. I mean, he doesn't know I took it."

A few exasperated "Oh, come ons" and "Jesus Fucking Christs" escaped from the crowd.

"Let me get this straight," the clerk said. "You are trying to get a *stolen* truck out of the impound yard? Without a license?" The man started laughing. "This is a first."

Melanie started laughing too. Lizzie might've as well if Kyle didn't look like he was about to cry.

"Listen," Lizzie said, "he's not lying."

"Miss, even if he's not, there's nothing I can do. I can't release a truck except to its rightful owner."

Kyle gritted his teeth. Lizzie figured there must be more to the story. She wanted to make *some* progress for him. "Can you at least tell us what we owe?"

"For a truck that isn't yours?"

"Come on, Lizzie," Melanie said, "let's get out of here."

"Yes," Lizzie replied, looking at Kyle. "You want to know what you owe, right? So you can call your *friend*?" Lizzie nodded at Kyle, a cue. "Right?"

"It's not stolen. I swear."

The man shook his head. "Whose name would the truck be

under?"

"Jimmy's. James McDermott." Kyle faked a smile. "He's a family friend. A *good* family friend. Who lets me *borrow* his truck any time I want. I forgot to tell him this time, and I don't want him to find out I got it towed—"

The man behind the glass held up one hand, clacking away at the keys with the other.

"Got some bad news for you, son. Says here that truck was picked up by…your good family friend, James McDermott… fifteen minutes ago."

Stuck in traffic trying to get on the Bay Bridge, Jimmy gnawed on his cigarette, pissed off over this unexpected detour. Orange construction signs flashed ahead, bottlenecking flow. A matter of time until the police started looking for him, if they weren't already. Which was why he was heading east. Everyone would expect him to flee south. Because everyone flees south. Jimmy would stay a step ahead, outthink the bastards. Get a few miles off the grid. He knew a place in Tracy where he could swap the truck for a new ride.

He wasn't paranoid. But he wasn't a moron either. Morons don't have a hundred thousands dollars sitting beside them in a brown backpack, which he patted, momentarily pleased, before seething again. The little shit dragged him down to the city and made him risk his freedom by strutting into an impound yard run by the county. As in The Law. Forget that bullshit about "authorized tow service provider." That's all it was, a big racket for police to swoop and seize private property, make a buck off the little guy's back. Fucking Kyle. He'd told Deke that kid was trouble. Deke wouldn't listen. Look at all the good it did him.

A long line of cars and buses ebbed beneath granite gray ramps. Who does bridge construction on a Sunday? Fucking city. This was why Jimmy lived up north. In the country with its wide open air. Couldn't stand this place. Goddamn bums with cardboard signs, asking for *his* money. Spare change? What was that? Money he didn't need? Jimmy hadn't had jack his whole life, but he wouldn't be caught dead sitting in shit-stained trousers, begging for quarters. When it came to luck, Jimmy made his own. He felt for his gun.

Jimmy pulled off, flipped a bitch on Bryant. Maybe he should double back, take city streets out of town, hit the San Mateo Bridge. Better yet, find a used car lot in South City. The sooner he ditched this truck the better. Humungous gas-guzzler in this eco-friendly horseshit town was an invitation to get pulled over.

Kyle slumped against the brick wall, knees up, head in hands. Same place Raf and his merry band of losers had found him. Except now it was in front of the one person he wanted to impress. Couldn't have gone worse in there. It confirmed what Melanie had been saying about him all along. And the worst part was, she was right. He *was* a loser. Tow yard must've called Jimmy. Who wasn't dead after all. Maybe Jimmy had been on his heels the entire time. What did it matter now? The money was gone. A part of him knew he should have been relieved. That cash was trouble. No one was going to let him have that much money. But he wasn't relieved. If he'd learned one thing from Deke: money was hard to come by in this life, and it's worse when you're poor white trash from Dormundt. Deke had scrambled his whole life to make ends meet. Look at the good it did him. And as much as Kyle wanted to find his dad, he understood the reality of the situation, how fantastic, improbable that was. Even if he made it to Los Angeles, Kyle had no guarantees his father would be happy to see him. So many years had passed. Would his dad think he was some con artist trying to cash in? Regardless, his dad was there. And he was here. And that money? That money had been right in his hands. He could see it, feel it, smell it. That backpack was Kyle's best shot to get a leg up. He didn't have a penny in his pocket. Is that how guys like Raf end up the way they do? Opportunity knocks once. And the door slams shut.

He could hear Lizzie and Melanie arguing fifteen feet away, their voices escalating. He felt bad for Lizzie, who was still trying to stick up for him. Trying to retrieve a stolen car? Without a license? Christ, he *was* an idiot.

Kyle wished Lizzie would hurry up and walk away. Don't even say goodbye. Go and leave him in his misery. Listening to her try and defend him made him feel guilty on top of everything else.

The fighting stopped. He waited for footsteps to beat a path in the opposite direction. When he lifted his head, she was standing over him, an angry Melanie at her side.

"Tell me the truth, Kyle. One hundred percent truth, all right?"

He nodded.

"The money in the truck. Is it for real? Is it yours?"

"I swear to God. It belonged to my cousin, Deke. He…died. Now it belongs to me. As much as it belongs to anyone."

Lizzie pulled out her cell.

Melanie turned away, cursing under her breath.

"Tom," Lizzie said into her phone. "Yeah, it's me. I need you to do me a favor."

Jimmy was almost to the 101 South onramp when he saw the blues and reds flash in his rearview. Money on the seat. Gun tucked under his shirt. He had a decision to make, and not a lot of time to make it.

A time might come to draw on a cop. But not today.

Jimmy had walked out of what was essentially a police station storage lot, with stolen money from stolen pot that he'd found on a dead man. If they'd figured out who he was in the last twenty minutes, he was pretty much fucked anyway. Could be a brake light out.

Jimmy stashed the gun in the cushions, stowed the money back behind the seat where he'd found it, and pulled off to the side of Potrero Avenue. The gun was still within reach if necessary.

He watched in the side-view as the cop exited the squad car. Big fat fucker. No other cruisers. Please let this be a run-of-the-mill traffic stop.

Jimmy placed both hands on the wheel in plain view, flashing his best good-ol'-country-boy-lost-in-the-big-city smile.

"I help you officer?"

"License and registration."

Jimmy reached over, flipped down the glove compartment, grabbed his paperwork, pulled his wallet, slipping out his driver's license with steady hands. Don't act nervous. Got nothing to hide.

He passed them along. "Can you tell me what this is about? I'm not used to city driving—"

"Wait here," the cop said.

In the rearview, the cop leaned in his cruiser and grabbed the CB. Jimmy lit a cigarette, one hand drawing on the smoke, the other fingering the grip between the cushions.

A few moments later, the cop returned, hand on his firearm.

Fuck.

"You mind stepping from the vehicle, sir. Keep your hands where I can see them."

"Can you tell me—"

The cop unclipped the holster. "Sir. Now."

Jimmy unlocked his doors, nudged the driver's side open with his knee, exiting, hands high.

"Drop the cigarette. Turn around. Place your hands on the hood."

"Can you—"

"Turn around!"

Jimmy did as instructed, and the cop cuffed him, leading him back to the cruiser.

"We've had a report that a truck matching this description

was stolen."

"Wha—I just picked up the damn thing—my name is on the fucking registration. My license. That's *my* truck!"

"Watch your language, sir." The cop opened the back door. "Have a seat till we get to the bottom of this."

A couple minutes later, Lizzie's cell rang back. "Twenty-third and Potrero. Got it...Yes, I owe you." Lizzie slipped the phone in her pocket.

"What now?" Kyle asked.

"We go get your money."

Sitting in the back seat of Lizzie's car, Kyle still wasn't sure what was happening or how he was supposed to get his money, even after Lizzie explained the plan half a dozen times.

"I'm supposed to run up and what? Open the door? What if the money isn't there? What if the truck isn't there?"

"It's there," Lizzie said.

"Lizzie's ex-*boy*friend Tom is a computer whiz. He's already taking programming courses at Cal. They got like a billion scanners at their house."

"Tom hacked into the retrieval yard and police computer systems to report that the truck was stolen. Which alerted every cop in the city to stop Jimmy's truck if they saw it. They won't hold him long. Once his registration and license check out, they'll let him go."

"We had Tom do the same thing last summer to this asshole, Shawn O'Brien."

"You retrieved...property from his car?"

"No," Lizzie said. "Not that part."

"We reported his car stolen to fuck with him."

"He deserved it."

The girls laughed.

Lizzie steered beneath the underpass, crossing Division Street onto Potrero Avenue.

"I don't know what I'm supposed to do," Kyle said.

Melanie spun around. "Listen. Lizzie's sticking her neck out for you. Don't fuck this up."

"What if the doors are locked?"

Lizzie shrugged.

"How long till they figure out the truck isn't stolen?"

"Will you stop being such a pussy?" Melanie said. "What do you want us to do? Hold your hand and walk you up there?"

"Jimmy's going to see me."

Lizzie hooked a right on Twenty-first, then a quick left on Hampshire, circling back up to Twenty-third, where they could see the glow of police lights swirling. She set the car in park a block away.

"If they suspect Jimmy stole the truck," Lizzie said, "they'll have him sitting in the back of the cruiser."

"But it's not stolen. It's *his* truck. They'll figure that out sooner than later."

"Then you better hurry." Lizzie caught his eyes in the rearview, a smile curled on her lips.

Kyle exited and crept through a weed-sprouted lot, sticking to shadows. He saw Jimmy in the back of the cruiser, a cop on the radio. There was no way he could walk up to the truck without a distraction. He'd be a sitting duck. Which was when Lizzie steered past, pulling up on the curb of Twenty-third, shielding him from the cruiser's line of sight.

What was she doing? She'd put on her high school's jacket, pair of wolves on the back, twirling a finger through her hair, walking up to the cop...like she was flirting with him. Kyle heard her say something about being lost, as a long bus ground to a halt, gears groaning like a train pulling into the station. It was now or never.

Kyle crouched low, scooting to the truck's passenger's side. Just playing a game of solider, capture the flag, like he'd done as a boy with Deke a hundred times in the Mendocino wilds.

Please be unlocked please be unlocked please be unlocked...

CHAPTER TWENTY

Jimmy figured this day might end in the back of a squad car. But not over some bogus stolen truck rap. Jimmy had spent most his life stealing. Of course he'd get collared for something he didn't do, the one damn thing he paid for.

The cop had been talking into his radio, standing in front of the car when a girl approached. Young. But not too young. Underage but hot. Certainly fuckable. Smoking little body on her, from what he could tell. She had a bulky jacket wrapped around her. Boy was she working it. All she needed were the pigtails and lollipop. Gave Jimmy a goddamn chubby just sitting there. What did she want? A giant bus rumbled to a stop. The windows were up in the cruiser, so he couldn't hear much, cars whipping by, pedestrians breezing past. Then the bus lumbered off, and he caught sight of the two wolves on her back as she strolled away, got in her Lexus, and drove off.

The cop returned and apologized for the misunderstanding. Sorry, wrong truck. He helped Jimmy out, took off the cuffs, hopped in the cruiser, and was gone. Jimmy stood on the side of the road in the cloud of dust. What the hell had that been about?

Rubbing his wrists, Jimmy walked back to his truck. Maybe it was a legit stop. Bad info, worse timing. All good in the end though, right?

Second he sat down, it hit him.

Jimmy flipped around, searching for the backpack, even though he knew it wouldn't be there.

* * *

"See?" Kyle said, out of breath, tilting the open backpack for Melanie's benefit. "Told you I wasn't lying."

"Holy shit," Lizzie said. "How much is in there?"

"I don't know the exact amount. I didn't get the chance to count it before they towed the truck."

"Have you lost your fucking mind, Lizzie? It's stolen!"

"It's not stolen," Kyle said.

"Right. Because people cart around stacks of hundred-dollar bills. In a fucking backpack."

Melanie had a point. Lizzie had gotten swept up in the moment. Her mother always said she could be an actress, possessed a flair for the dramatic. Calling in a favor, setting up a sting, pretending to flirt with the cop to distract him as her partner retrieved the goods. It was a role. Even rocking the schoolgirl uniform by throwing on Tom's old varsity jacket—all men love the naughty schoolgirl look—like something out of a movie. But now reality was sinking in. It wasn't a good feeling.

"Where do you want to go, Mel?"

"With you two? Um. Nowhere."

"You want me to...drop you off somewhere?"

"Yeah. How about the next fucking street corner."

"You sure? I can bring you back to your car? Or your house?"

"I'd rather catch the fucking BART." Melanie glowered at Kyle. "I don't want to be anywhere near you guys when that redneck fucker comes back for his money."

"It's not *his* money."

"Well, it sure as shit isn't yours."

Lizzie guided the car across the intersection of Twenty-fourth and parked outside the BART station, and Melanie jumped out.

"Be careful," she said to Lizzie, before rushing down the stairs to catch a train.

Lizzie glanced over at Kyle, who was still beaming.

What had she gotten herself into?

* * *

Marcos had taken shit from pissed-off customers all day and was ready for a break. Even as the clock slogged down, one more guy had to come straggling in. How was it Marcos' fault that these scofflaws chose to park illegally instead of ponying up the twenty bucks for a lot?

The man approached his window. Sleeveless flannel shirt, blue jeans, cowboy boots. Out of towner.

"What can I do for you?" Marcos said, trying to sound cheerful. This was the point hammered home by his supervisors. Be empathetic, be compassionate, be kind.

"My name's Jim McDermott. I picked up my truck earlier." He looked over the other windows, which were empty.

The name sounded familiar but Marcos couldn't place where he'd heard it.

"I'm afraid my little brother might try to get it out too. He was the one who got it towed. Took it without my permission."

That's where Marcos had encountered the name. That weird kid who tried to pay for a stolen car without a license. This story made more sense. "Yeah, he was here," Marcos said, laughing. "He said the truck belonged to a family friend."

"That sounds like Kyle."

Marcos nodded. "That's right, Kyle. Told him you'd already picked it up." Marcos looked over at the empty seat where his coworker had been. "Was there—?"

McDermott thumbed outside, where a shiny red truck sat. "I was going to head back home but thought I oughtta come down here first, clear this up. Just in case. Didn't want Kyle getting in trouble for stealing my truck. I shouldn't say that though. Stealing. He's my baby brother. Not like I'd press charges or anything."

Marcos glanced up at the clock, feeling his stomach revolt. "No harm, no foul." He moved to shut the window but McDermott reached out, a gentle stop.

"The thing is, between me and you…"

"Marcos."

"The thing is, Marcos, my baby brother's been behaving strange. We're not from here. We live up by Eureka, tiny town. Kyle keeps acting out. Taking cars that don't belong to him. Running down to the city. Getting in trouble. He's got this new girlfriend. I think she's bad news. Was she here, too?"

Marcos recalled the young girl who was with him. There were two girls, but the boy only had eyes for the one. "Yeah, she was here."

"Teenagers, eh?"

"Like I said, no worries on this end."

"You catch a name?"

"Name?"

"The girl. With my brother. You get her name?"

"You don't know your brother's girlfriend's name?"

"Like I said. Acting crazy. Lots of different girls."

"I'm not sure how I can help you," Marcos said, remembering something. "Hold on." He reached into his desk. "She left her credit card." He stopped.

"You can keep the credit card," McDermott said with a smile, "I just want to check on my baby brother."

Marcos thought for a moment. He'd heard a lot of strange pleas at the impound yard, and was used to people trying to scam the system. This one didn't seem to have any angle, not that he could see.

"Elizabeth," he said, reading the name beside the Chase logo, before tucking the card back in the drawer.

"Elizabeth," Jim repeated. "That's right. What's her last name again?"

"I'm sorry. I can't give that information out."

"Why not? Her car wasn't in here, was it?"

"Well, no. She—"

"What? Gave you her credit card to get out *my* truck? A credit card you kept."

"I told you she left it by mistake—"

For an instant, something sinister flashed in the man's eyes, a seething malice Marcos couldn't comprehend.

Then the rage vanished and Jim McDermott was all smiles again. "No worries. All good." He slapped the counter, thanked Marcos for his time, and was out the door.

Marcos stared down at his hands, which trembled. He'd been on the receiving end of worse. Berated, threatened. Police escorts off impound grounds were not uncommon. But as he watched the man climb in his red truck and drive away, Marcos couldn't recall ever having felt more relieved when a customer left.

He was hungry, stir crazy from the cubicle. His coworker, Ignacio, returned from break. Marcos didn't recall seeing McDermott in here earlier, so he must've retrieved the truck from Ignacio. It was just the two of them on Sunday. For a moment, Marcos thought of asking him about the man. Then decided against it. The matter was closed, and it had nothing to do with him. He locked up his station, plucked his keys, and shut his drawer, reminding himself to call the credit card company after his break was over.

Stupid wetback fuck. Should've closed that window on his neck and beaten it out of him. Jimmy had sat outside, watching, waiting till that other dumb shit returned from his break. Couldn't run the same con twice. And all he had to go on was a generic first name. Great.

Why was she helping Kyle? One of those bored richies looking for a thrill? If she had her own credit card at that age, must have money. Girl couldn't have been more than eighteen. Must be still in high school...

The car.

Girls who drive a Lexus don't go to public schools.

He remembered the wolves.

CHAPTER TWENTY-ONE

The Salks lived on the opposite end of town, far from the squalid Highway, high on the hill. This short stretch of mountain road, called The Arlington, would've been considered the better side of the tracks if trains ran through places like Dormundt. Their giant wood house looked more like a rustic log cabin than it did a big city mansion, but make no mistake: the family enjoyed financial luxury, parading it above the rest of the tinderboxes in the flats. For those who had nothing, must be hard to look up and see that all day long.

"Let me do the talking," Jacobs said. "No offense. But you can come off as—"

"What?"

"Abrasive."

Ronnie Salk answered the door in his pajama pants, no shirt, soft belly drooping over sloppy knot drawstring. Jacobs already had his badge out. Ronnie squinted through his glasses.

"Detective Jacobs. This is my partner, Detective Nomura. We'd like to speak with you about your friend, Kyle. All right if we come in?"

Ronnie nodded and stepped aside.

The dark wood foyer led into an expansive kitchen. Large island in the middle, oversized plates stacked in see-through glass pantry, nothing out of place, nary a dirty dish or cup in sight. Jacobs ran his finger along the island marble. Not a speck of grease.

"Your parents home?" Jacobs asked.

Ronnie shook his head. "Napa. Won't be back till Monday."

"Not big on wine tasting, eh?" Jacobs joked. "I'm guessing you heard about the situation at the Skunk Train the other night?"

"Have you spoken with Kyle?" Nomura asked.

The boy pushed the glasses back on his nose and glanced around the room.

"Because if you have, you need to tell us. Your friend is in a lot of trouble—"

"Could I bother you for some coffee, Ronnie?"

Ronnie pointed at the whittled craftsman cupboard, and the shiny Jura Impressa Z7 below, gleaming like spit-shined chrome.

Jacobs pulled a robust bag of beans from the shelf. The canvas sack was tied off with twine. The label was not in English.

"This isn't that kopi luwak coffee, is it?"

"I don't know what that is."

"There's this type of cat, Ronnie." He turned to Nomura. "Have you heard about this?"

Nomura half-shrugged.

"Called an Asian palm civet. Lives on islands in the South Pacific. Indonesia, Bali, Philippines." Jacobs dumped dark beans into the burr grinder, hit the switch and watched the roasted seeds tumble through the tiny window as the little motor whirred. "Remarkable, these cats," he went on, toggling off and toppling fine dust into a cone. "They *love* coffee berries. These cats will scale trees and pick the branches clean, eat coffee cherries like they were candy." Jacobs turned on the maker and hot water hissed, coughing out the hose. He paused while the pot percolated. "The civet has a unique digestive system," Jacobs continued. "Like no other animal on Earth, and after they eat the beans—there's no polite way to say this, Ronnie—they shit the berry out, whole. Mug?"

Ronnie pointed at another cupboard while the pungent scent

of brewed coffee wafted over the kitchen.

"Before the civet shits out the berries, though, something extraordinary happens in its intestinal tract. Enzymes and amino acids, peptides—fermentation—this process turns ordinary berries into magic beans." Jacobs poured a piping hot cup. "Makes them very valuable. Very rare. In fact, kopi luwak coffee is the most expensive in the world. Crazy, huh? Sumatran farmers sift through cat shit, sift out seeds, and sell them to rich people all over the world." Jacobs took a sip and smacked his lips. "Goddamn, that's good coffee." He smiled at Ronnie, lowering his voice like he was sharing a secret. "Tell you the truth, Ronnie, coffee this good, I don't care if it came out a cat's ass."

"I don't think it's—"

"It's okay." Jacobs winked. "Our little secret. Have you spoken with Kyle?"

"He called me yesterday."

"When?" Nomura asked. "He tell you where he was? Where he was going?"

Jacobs turned around. "Would you mind getting that thing out of the car?"

"What thing?"

"The one in the car," he said, staring until Nomura took the hint and left them alone.

She had some decent instincts but her people skills sorely lacked; she knew nothing about making a witness feel comfortable, which was the name and game of interrogation.

"Listen, Ronnie, I could use your help. My partner misspoke. Kyle is not 'in trouble.' But we *would* like to talk to him. We know he was at the Skunk Train. After the events of that night, everyone's high strung, fingers getting itchy. People died at the motel. Cops shot at. Not good. I want to get to Kyle before anything bad happens. Know what I mean?"

Ronnie nodded.

"Anything you can tell me would be a big help."

"He wanted me to look up his uncle's address."

"His uncle?"

"On the internet. All I could find was an old San Francisco address on Jones Street."

"Kyle close with his uncle?"

Ronnie shook his head. "I think Kyle needs him to find his father."

"Kyle doesn't know where his dad lives?"

"Says he's a famous director in Hollywood."

"That true?"

"No. I don't know. I'm not sure Kyle even believes it. I think it's just a lie he's told himself for so long it's become real to him. If that makes sense."

"It does, Ronnie." Jacobs reached out and squeezed Ronnie's shoulder. "That's a big help." He set down the mug on the counter. "Thanks for the coffee."

They ordered sandwiches in a quiet café on Dolores Street, dreamy synth pop oozing out the sound system, late-afternoon fog rolling in over Twin Peaks, like it did almost every afternoon in San Francisco, wetting the windows. Between the concert and calling in favors, Lizzie hadn't found the time to eat. But nerves were killing her appetite.

Not Kyle, who sat opposite her, backpack by his side, scarfing a meatless burger, impervious to any danger. He'd also brought a shaving kit with him into the café, which he must've lifted from the truck, as well. Though Lizzie couldn't figure out why he needed a razor. Guy didn't even have peach fuzz.

Lizzie's house was less than a mile up the road, above Noe Valley, in the foothills of Diamond Heights. The only home she'd ever known, an architectural wonder and a residence millions would kill to live in. And right now it was last place she wanted to be.

Not that she was comfortable sitting here. What was she doing? Yeah, she liked Kyle, but she also understood the difference between fantasy and fucking up so bad you couldn't come back.

"What's next?" she asked.

"What do you mean?"

"Where are you going?"

"I'm getting out of here."

The barista, who was riding the vegan train hard, with the trademark sallow cheeks of someone who hadn't eaten a cheeseburger in over a decade, asked if they wanted anything else. Lizzie waved her off as The Cocteau Twins dripped Cherry Colored Funk and the girl tugged at her nose ring, before returning behind the bar.

Lizzie waited for a better answer.

"I'm going to find my father in Hollywood."

"I like you, Kyle." She could see him blush when she said that. It was cute. "But I can't go with you to L.A."

"I know that."

Lizzie caught his eye. "The money. Where'd it come from?"

"You think I stole it?"

Lizzie didn't answer right away. She wanted to say no. But she also didn't want to lie. "Think about how this looks," she whispered. "You have a backpack full of cash."

"You sound like your friend, Melanie."

"I know she can be rude. But, Kyle, it would look that way to *any*one."

"I thought you were different."

"From what? Someone having common sense?" Lizzie took his hand. "I'm here, aren't I? Tell me the truth. Where did you get the money?"

"My cousin."

"Your cousin."

"Deke."

"Who died?"

"That guy, with the truck? That's Jimmy. He *is* a friend. At least I thought he was. Him and Deke have…had…a business." Kyle leaned closer. "Selling weed. Everyone does it up in

Dormundt. Deke didn't push too much weight. He'd sell to a few regulars at the bar he worked at." Kyle polished the last of his sandwich, washing it down with his fizzy pink soda. "The other day he comes home, freaking out, says we have to leave. I ask what's up, but he's being all mysterious. Then he shows me two bags stuffed with skunk. Says he…found it."

"Found it. Where?"

"I don't know. Just that it had belonged to someone else."

"He stole it?"

"Deke's a good guy."

"Taking something that doesn't belong to you is still stealing. No matter how you justify it."

"Deke wasn't the strong-arm type. He was tough, but he wasn't jacking anyone up. Wasn't his style."

"What about Jimmy?"

Kyle shrugged.

"What happened next?"

"Deke wanted to make a quick turnaround. He and Jimmy set up a deal at the Skunk Train."

"Skunk Train?"

"It's a motel. Shithole. On the Dormundt Highway. Entire highway is about a mile long. Sort of a joke name. It was a set-up."

"Setup? By who?"

"Dirty cops. Bikers. Other dealers. How should I know? But it was bad. Everyone started shooting. I stayed in the room. Watched Deke get crushed by the semi. I didn't see Jimmy. Figured he was dead, too, so I grabbed his keys and took off."

"Are the cops looking for you?"

"I don't know. No one knows I was there."

"Except Jimmy."

"Except him, yeah. But it's not like he's going to call the police. He doesn't have a right to that money any more than I do."

"So where did the money come from?"

"Beats me. I didn't even know the backpack was there until I went to fill the tank a couple hours later. Must've made the exchange beforehand. It was sitting in the bed." He scratched his head. "It's a gray area."

"A gray area?"

"Yeah. Who the money belongs to. A gray area. But I know if Deke was still alive he'd want me to have it. I appreciate all you did for me. I don't need you to drop me at the bus station or anything. I can get there on my own." He looked out the window into the wall of clouds. "Which way to the bus station?"

Lizzie twisted her mouth, trying to gauge how deep in she was.

"Jimmy doesn't know who you are. He couldn't find his ass with both hands, and there's no way he can find me. The truck was our connection. If I knew he was still alive, believe me, I wouldn't have been driving around in it. I know you think I'm some dumb kid."

"I don't think you're a dumb kid."

"Sure you do. It's okay. Everyone in Dormundt thinks the same thing. But I'm the one sitting here with the money, on my way to Hollywood. So who's laughing now?"

"To Hollywood. To find your famous director dad."

"I know how it sounds. But I'm telling you the truth."

Lizzie sighed. "C'mon. I'll drop you off at the bus station."

Kyle thought Dormundt got gray. It did, but nothing like San Francisco. The constant fog made Kyle feel like he was in one of those old movies Kristy and Deke used to make him watch on boring Friday nights, back when they were still dating and trying to act like parents. At the time he'd protest and complain how lame it was. Right now he'd give all that money back to be sitting with Deke and Kristy, watching an old movie in the trailer.

Lizzie asked him a few polite questions as they steered past murky produce stands as Mexican shopkeepers battened hatches, the day drawing to a close. Kyle gave his answers, clipped, single-word responses. He knew he was sulking and that he should put on a brave face. But the first pretty girl who seemed to genuinely like him was about to walk out of his life forever. He wasn't in the mood to be gracious.

As they crossed beneath an underpass, Lizzie's phone buzzed.

She slid it on, reading the text as she drove, casual, her expression unchanged. She set down the cell, swerving to catch the freeway onramp south.

"Changed my mind. I'm feeling a road trip."

CHAPTER TWENTY-TWO

It was amazing how stupid kids were today. Starved-for-attention, dopey girls. They put everything online. Their whole damn lives. Forget posting pictures of themselves looking like ducks or half-dressed sluts, mugging for the camera with a belt for a skirt; they included every bit of their personal, private information, splashed it across cyberspace for the whole wide world web to see. No wonder creeps thrived in the city. Even a "smart" girl like this Lizzie Decker. That's what she went by. Lizzie. Not Elizabeth. Elizabeth was her mother. Not bad looking though, that one. A bit old for Jimmy's tastes. But still...

Following a brief visit inside an internet café, armed with nothing but a first name, loose physical description, and private school mascot, Jimmy had an address. The dad's charity, The Bridges and Hands Foundation, helped as much as anything. Once he stumbled across that, he was in like Flynn. Besides providing the name of the parents, the webpage showcased plenty of pics. Lizzie dolled up at fundraisers, toasting at galas. Other unstaged shots, too. No doubt she'd inherited mom's genes. Girl was a knockout, that natural, roll-out-of-bed beauty that drove Jimmy wild. Kind of girl who didn't need makeup. Slap on a tee and a tight pair of faded blues and call it a day. What the hell was she doing with a turdbuglar like Kyle? Then it was a simple matter of a White Pages search.

Jimmy had heard of guys making a killing stealing identities, credit card fraud, even some dumbasses printing checks to themselves with stolen corporate accounts, which spelled a sure-fire prison rap. It had always seemed beyond his rudimentary hunting-and-pecking cyber skills, but fuck if it was this easy to find where a stranger lived perhaps he'd give identity theft a try.

The address listed Diamond Heights. There was one route in, winding postcard streets peppered with baby strollers, bistros, and tiny dogs. The fog had grown thicker by the time he pulled in front of the house, a jarring giant glass rectangle, a post-modern nightmare. Would pass for a museum up in Dormundt. If they had things like museums or culture up in Dormundt. Down here, it was just another monstrosity among monstrosities. He didn't see Lizzie's Lexus. A big ol' soccer mom SUV was parked in the turnaround driveway, porch lights blazing as if expecting company.

Jimmy parked on the street, contemplating how to play it. He could wait for Kyle and the girl to come home. Assuming a girl like Lizzie would bring a farm boy mutherfucker like Kyle home to meet the parents. Which was a resounding no in Jimmy's opinion.

Grabbing his gray work coat from the back, Jimmy decided to try his luck glad-handing. The bullshit "worried about my brother" excuse had worked twice already. Let's try for the hat trick. Up until now, Jimmy had figured Kyle would make for Hollywood and Daddy Dearest, but that was before he learned the girl was involved. Either way, Jimmy wanted to gather as much intel as possible. L.A. sprawled over half the desert.

Hard to believe a girl with a life like this would piss it away on a jaghole runt like Kyle. Then again, rich girls slum it all the time, makes 'em feel worldly, superior. Besides the philanthropy, Dave Decker logged hours as an investment consultant. Jimmy knew these corporate A-types; he'd sold plenty of dope to them. Driven to succeed at all costs, captains of industry horseshit. Emotionally absent mother, meek and submissive, girl starved for attention. A picture began to take shape.

But right away Dave and Elizabeth's behavior threw him for

a loop. The mother made sense. Jimmy had picked the wrong cliché, is all. The father, though…

"Forgive us for being so forward," Elizabeth asked him. "But are you Lizzie's…boyfriend?"

Lady, Jimmy wanted to say, I'm twenty-nine years old, slathered in ink, and sling dope for a living. What kind of mother would let her teenage daughter date someone like me? But he bit his tongue.

They were seated in the living room, on microsuede sofas, beneath a large splatter painting that resembled an inferior third grader's artwork.

"We try not to interfere in our daughter's personal life," Elizabeth Decker said.

Maybe you should.

A part of Jimmy needed to make them squirm. His old man wasn't worth shit, but at least the bastard took him fishing once in a while. No way either of these two was touching a worm.

"No," Jimmy said. "I'm not Lizzie's boyfriend. She's dating my younger brother. Kyle." Jimmy waited for recognition, but if they'd heard the name before, they weren't letting on. "He's missing. He's done this in the past, stayed away a couple nights, but Mom is concerned."

"How old is your brother?"

"Fifteen." Jimmy was taking a stab. Little shit didn't have his license, he knew that much.

"I'm sorry," Elizabeth said, "but I don't believe your brother is with Lizzie. We saw her this morning."

"Last night," Dave corrected her.

"Yes, last night."

What was up with these two? They kept averting eyes, fiddling with buttons, tapping toes, but Jimmy didn't get the impression it had anything to do with him. What did he care? One of them probably got caught having an affair; that's what the rich and spineless do to fend off the boredom. Must be so difficult being able to afford whatever kind of cheese you want without looking at the price tag. Truth was, Jimmy hadn't been able to figure out why they'd opened the door to a guy like him in the first place.

"What did you say your name was?" Elizabeth asked.

"Jimmy."

"And your brother?"

"Kyle."

Dave and Elizabeth returned to making faces at each other.

"I don't know what else we can tell you," Elizabeth said. "But I don't think our daughter could be dating your brother."

"Why's that?" Jimmy knew why of course, but people like her never wanted to offend to a person's face. He might be poor white trash, but these San Francisco liberal fucks liked to pretend they gave a shit about people like him. He'd make her say it.

But it was Dave who stepped up. "It's that Lizzie tends to date...older boys."

"Well, she's dating Kyle now. I know for a fact she saw him today."

"Did you see her? Talk to her? Is she all right?"

"No, man, I didn't talk to her."

"Where did you say you lived again?"

"Up north."

"And how did your brother and Lizzie meet?"

"I don't know. Same way anybody meets. Bar, club, whatever."

"Isn't fifteen too young to get into bars?"

"Could say the same about a girl still in high school." Jimmy had seen the photos on her Facebook page, half of which show-cased glitzy neon clubs, cocktail in hand. "Look, I don't know how they met. But they did and they have been spending a lot of time together. Think you can call Lizzie? See if my brother is with her?"

Dave held up a hand and Elizabeth excused herself, leaving the men to talk.

"I'll be frank, Jimmy. This isn't a good time."

"So you can't call her?"

"It's not that. She won't pick up."

"How do you know?"

"Because I've been trying all day. We had a fight last night. Family stuff. And she's mad at us. I've been trying nonstop and haven't been able to get through. I just sent her a text when you were at the door, in fact. Nothing." Dave panned over at his wife, who fiddled with baking dishes as if she were preparing to cook instead of instructing the chef on what to prepare. "Her friend, Melanie, might be able to help you. I can give you her cell." Dave pulled his phone. "I don't know if she'll answer either. She works Sunday evenings, I believe."

"Where?"

"Where what?"

"Where does she work? In case she doesn't answer."

It had been a long day, and Marcos Rivas was glad it was over. Next to maybe being a meter maid, no city employee was despised more than the lowly tow yard operator. Eight hours of being yelled at and spat on was a lousy way to make a living.

Walking across the dark parking lot to his battered gray two-door, he heard car doors slam behind him, and turned to find two men, one black, one white, exiting a Crown Vic and heading his way.

The bigger of the two flashed a badge.

"I'm Carter. This is my partner, Banks. You have a minute?"

Banks fished around his inside pocket. He extracted a picture and held it up. "You recognize this man?"

Marcos nodded. The guy from earlier, the one with the missing brother, the backwoods smooth talker with the short fuse. He knew something didn't seem right about the guy. "Got his truck out of impound earlier this afternoon."

Banks thumbed through the chain link, toward the office. "Other guy tells us he came back from break and saw you two talking. Can you tell us what about?"

"His brother."

"Brother?"

"Said he was looking for him."

"You remember the brother's name?"

"Kyle. He'd come in earlier, too. Kid was trying to get the truck out. No license. Registered to someone else. Who's dumb enough to try to retrieve a stolen truck from impound?" Marcos pointed at the photo Banks still held. "Turns out the truck belonged to that guy, his brother."

"How long ago was this?"

"The kid?" Marcos thought. "Maybe noon."

"Was he alone?"

"No," Marcos said. "Had a couple girls with him."

"You get their names?"

Damn. Marcos remembered in the bustle and aggravation of the evening that he'd forgotten to call the credit card company.

"What is it?"

"One of the girls, Elizabeth...Decker...she left her credit card. She'd put it down to pay for the truck before I explained I couldn't release it to them. Forgot to take it with her. I meant to call the credit card company. Guess I got sidetracked. Weekends are a headache around here. People go out drinking, park on the median, sober up, pissed they got towed. Come down here, yell at me—"

"You still have this card?" Carter asked.

"The drawer at my station." The last thing Marcos felt like doing was trudging back across the long, damp lot to the office. But he already knew he was going to have to. "I suppose you want me to get it?"

"That would be helpful."

Marcos thought of something else.

"Spit it out," said Banks.

"The other guy. In the picture."

"McDermott."

"He was real talky, friendly, too. At first. Then he got kind of…mean. Maybe I shouldn't have…"

"It's all right. Tell us."

"He gave me this sob story about his brother, blaming it all on the girlfriend. But he didn't know her name. I had the card, so I told him. Just her first name. Gave me a funny feeling after I did it."

"How so?"

"Weird he wouldn't know his own brother's girlfriend's name, no?"

CHAPTER TWENTY-THREE

An hour out of the city, the night warmed like it was actually summer for a change. Seasons didn't matter in San Francisco. You had about two weeks of heat, three months of rain, and the rest of the time was a crapshoot.

"What are you doing?" Lizzie asked.

Kyle fished around his shaving kit. "I think I have some pot in here."

"Sweet. You could've mentioned that earlier."

"Forgot I even had it until now, trust me."

Kyle fired the half-joint as scenery zipped past, stripped down valley on one side, swelling meadow on the other. Windmills perched high atop fields of swaying burnt grasses. He took a good, long toke, before passing it along to Lizzie. "Can I ask you something?"

"I hate that."

"What?"

"That question. It's stupid. 'Can I ask you something?' What if I say no?"

"Then I wouldn't ask you."

Lizzie peered over. He wasn't trying to be clever. He really wanted permission first.

"Okay," she said. "You may ask me your question."

"Why did you change your mind? I'm glad you did—this beats a Greyhound—but...?"

"Why did I decide to drive a guy I barely know, who admitted stealing pot and money—"

"I told you I didn't steal it— " Then Kyle saw Lizzie grinning, messing with him.

"I don't know. You needed to get to SoCal. I didn't feel like going home. The highway was right there. I guess I wanted to do something...unexpected. What's it matter?" She passed the joint back to Kyle. "Maybe," Lizzie said, "I didn't want to say goodbye yet."

"I'll give you some of it."

"What? The money? I don't need your money, Kyle."

"Must be nice."

"Money's not everything."

"Maybe not when you have it." Kyle formed his hands into a rectangle, miming a dollar bill. "Moves mountains." He re-sparked the joint. "I can't even afford a junker car."

"You can now," she said, smiling. A second later: "I thought you didn't have your license?"

"I don't. But Dormundt's got a population of about twelve. I'd drive Deke's truck when he wasn't around. Nobody complains up there."

"You getting homesick?"

"Hell no. It's where I'm from, though. Never been away this long. And—"

"What?"

"I'm realizing Deke's not coming back. Like, ever. Of course he's not. He's dead. But I'm finally...feeling it. It sucks. I wasn't very nice to him. And he tried, and I made things harder. Or at least I didn't help the situation."

Lizzie pointed at the glove compartment. "Want to grab my iPod out of there? Find the Connells. *One Simple Word*. Old school. Good road trip music."

"Never heard of them."

"What do you listen to?"

Kyle shrugged. "Whatever Deke had on. Country mostly. Girls without makeup in blue jeans. Pickups. Crying in your beer. That kind of stuff."

"Okay. But what do *you* like? Music, man, it's personal. Can't adopt someone else's taste. It has to…speak to your soul, resonate. Hit you here." Lizzie poked her heart.

"I like Springsteen. I write sometimes. His words make sense."

"Bruce Springsteen?" She stifled a laugh.

"What's wrong with Bruce Springsteen?"

"Nothing. If you're forty." She wiggled her fingers. "Come on, grandpa. Hand me the iPod."

The boutique bell's dinging surprised Melanie. The first customer she'd had all night. Delicate Discoveries' location didn't invite window shoppers. The tiny boutique catered to petit woman's fashions, which didn't help in the Castro. At least if you carried the bigger sizes, you'd get the drag queens.

Once Melanie saw the man standing in the doorway, she knew who he was, and what he wanted. She felt for her phone. She'd been texting Jax about hitting a club later since Lizzie was MIA. She couldn't feel it on the counter and didn't want to look and be obvious.

"Hi," Melanie said in her best salesgirl voice, swallowing. "Can I help you find something?"

The man stroked silky merchandise on a rack, rubbing forefinger and thumb over see-through sheer. "Yeah," he said in a high girly voice, "I'm looking for a bra and panty set." He held up a thong. "Think this will fit me?" He dropped it to the floor. "Cut the shit, Melanie. Where's my fucking money."

"I don't know what you're talking about."

He turned and flipped the sign to closed, twirled the stick, shut the slatted blinds, locked the door. He killed the lights, and the tiny shop fell dark, yellow streetlamp slicing through the cracks.

He took a step toward Melanie, who retreated against the counter.

"Let's try this again. What's my name?"

"Jimmy."

"Good girl. You were down the impound with your rich bitch friend Lizzie, and that little shit, Kyle, trying to get *my* truck."

"It wasn't my idea. I didn't know—"

"Don't fuck with me, Melanie. I had a shit-ton of money in that truck. Until you and the other two musketeers pulled that stunt with the cop. By the way, for shits and giggles, how did you manage that?"

"Lizzie's ex's dad is a hotshot lawyer in the city. Tom's got all these police scanners and computers, figured out how to hack into the system a while ago."

"Cute. Future of fucking America." Jimmy loomed over Melanie. She could smell his cigarette breath and unwashed stink, all man musk. "I'm glad you're not lying to me, Melanie. You don't know the favor you're doing yourself. What did Kyle tell you about me?"

"Nothing. Just that you were a family friend and that the money belonged to his cousin, who's dead, so now it's his."

"The little shit said that? Sprouting some fuzz on those tiny balls of his. What you think of him?"

"Kyle? Nothing. He's weird and a liar."

Jimmy flung his arm around her, laughing. "You're a bright girl, Mel. I like you. We're going to get along fine. Now tell me where they're going?"

"I don't know."

"Mel," Jimmy said, sounding disappointed. "And you were doing so well."

"It's the truth. After they took the money, I told them to let me off at BART and I haven't talked to her since."

Jimmy bent down and stared into her eyes, like he could see her true intentions behind them. He plucked her cell off the countertop six inches from her fingertips and flipped it to her.

"Call her."

"Lizzie?"

"Yes. Find out where she is."

Melanie went to punch the speed dial but Jimmy stopped her.

"Just know, even though I like you, you try anything, like hint that I'm here, give some secret code bullshit, I'll break your fucking teeth, okay? Nothing personal. But I will hurt you if I have to."

"You don't have to threaten me. Lizzie's the one who got herself into this mess."

Funny how fast a bad hand can turn in your favor. Last night had been one of the worst nights of Kyle's life, those perverts and getting his ass handed to him by a punk like Raf, sleeping like a dirty dog in a bush, no money, no one to call, a future bleak, hopeless, and now here he was sitting next to the prettiest girl he'd ever met, driving away scot-free with all the money he'd ever need, on the open highway, shimmering guitars and sweet melodies, heading to Hollywood to see his dad. Life was a pretty sweet fruit.

Lizzie's cell chirped.

"Melanie," she said.

Lizzie turned down the stereo, cutting off the singer, who was crooning about needing a gun and the dangers of being a pilot.

"Oh, hi, Mel." Lizzie rolled her eyes at Kyle. "Nothing." Pause. "I'm taking him to Hollywood."

Kyle zoned out. He didn't need to hear this. Words filtered in. *Because she wanted to. Because it was none of her business.* Then the call ended.

"She hang up on you?"

"Either that or we got cut off."

"I hate to tell you this, but your friend isn't very nice."

"We've been best friends since kindergarten."

"We don't always make the best decisions at five years old."

The cell chirped again and Lizzie picked up.

"Are you going to hang up on me—what?" Lizzie grabbed her purse, fishing till she found her wallet, flipping it open. "Damn."

"What's wrong?"

Lizzie cupped the cell. "I left my credit card at the impound. Guy phoned Melanie." She returned to the call. "Almost Monterey...you don't need to do that. I think we have enough money." She glanced at Kyle. "I can use my ATM...I guess...if you want to...okay...The Driftwood?...You remember *that*?" Lizzie giggled. "Thanks, Mel." She clicked off the phone.

"What's up?"

"Melanie's going to bring me the credit card."

"Why? We have plenty of cash."

"We're only a couple hours south of the city. Plus, I'm not sure you want to start spending any of that yet."

"Why not?"

"What if it's traceable or something?"

"It's not traceable."

"I think Melanie feels bad for how she acted and wants to apologize."

"To me? I don't care."

"She's my best friend. I've known her forever. She reminded me of the hotel my father used to take us to. The Driftwood. We were like sisters back then. This one time...never mind. Besides, it's late. I don't feel like getting to L.A. in the middle of the night and trying to find a hotel. Let's get a fresh start in the morning. Have you ever been to Monterey?"

Kyle shook his head.

"You've never seen the aquarium? Oh, you'll love it. My dad used to bring me all the time. Cannery Row? John Steinbeck? The author?"

"I don't read much."

"You told me you like to write."

"I do. But I don't like to read."

"You can't write if you don't read, Kyle." She shook her head with feigned disappointment. "So much to learn."

* * *

"You did good," Jimmy said, plucking the cell from her hand, and tucking it in his back pocket.

"Hey, I need that!"

"I'm sure you can buy another one."

"No, I can't. I'm not like Lizzie. I don't have rich parents who pay for everything and give me whatever I want. I have to work. That phone's over three hundred dollars."

"I'll drop it in the mail when I'm done."

"Not good enough. I helped you out. Now you're fucking me over."

Could Jimmy afford to piss off Melanie? Once he was gone, what would stop her from calling Lizzie, or her parents, or the cops? Threats only go so far if you're not willing to back them up. Jimmy had done a lot of fucked-up shit in his life, but he'd never hit a woman. Threatened to all the time, sure, who hasn't?

"Come on," he said. "We're going."

"Where?"

"To see the fishes."

Across the street, a car waited in the shadows, staking out the boutique, no one saying a word, all eyes focused on the man and girl as they climbed into the red truck.

The Mexican turned over the engine, ebbed forward, and followed.

CHAPTER TWENTY-FOUR

Kristy Miller walked in the door, dropping yesterday's mail on the table, along with her teacher's bag, overstuffed with book reports, which she'd taken out of town to grade. She never got around to it. She stared down the long night ahead of her. A glass of wine would make it more bearable.

In the pantry, she pulled the last bottle of St. Francis from the crate of wine they'd purchased last year when she managed to drag Deke wine tasting. Kristy wasn't much of a drinker, and Deke wasn't the kind of guy who did wine tastings. But she'd gotten free tickets, and he'd been a good sport, even taking her on the vineyard gondola. Deke didn't go for that romantic stuff, but he was sweet that day. He tried. In his own way.

This past weekend had been rough for Kristy. When she heard the news from Jimmy, she couldn't stomach going back home alone. She got on the highway and drove the five hours to see her sister in Medford.

Even though they'd been apart when he died, Kristy had always planned on being with Deke. Once he gave up the pot dealing, curbed his temper, grew up, left behind bad influences like Jimmy. It felt like they were taking a break, and one day they'd pick up where they left off. Kristy didn't throw around words like "soul mate," but she knew they belonged together. Despite his rough exterior, Deke had a huge, giving heart. What he'd done for Kyle, taking him in when his father didn't want him, proved that. And now he was gone.

A loud knock startled Kristy. She set down the bottle and made her way to the front door, where a man and a woman stood.

"Kristy Miller?" The man held up a badge. "I'm Detective Jacobs. This is my partner, Detective Nomura. Can we come in?"

Kristy pushed open the screen.

"If you're here about Deke," she said, "I already heard."

"From the news?" Detective Nomura asked.

"From his friend, Jimmy. Yesterday morning."

Jacobs gazed around her place. "We have a few questions, if you don't mind. We stopped by earlier, but you weren't here."

"I went to see my sister in Oregon." Kristy pointed to the kitchen. "Can I get you anything?"

"Whatever you're having is fine," Jacobs said.

"I was about to pour a glass of wine."

"We're okay then. You know bosses. They frown upon drinking on the job." He winked. "But, please, don't let us stop you."

Kristy was glad he said that.

"I have to be back to work tomorrow," she called from the kitchen. "This has been very hard."

Jacobs followed her. When she had difficulty with the corkscrew, he stepped in. "Here, let me."

"What do you want to know?" Kristy asked as he poured a generous glass. This was not how she wanted to spend her Sunday evening, rehashing regrets with the police.

"Do you know where McDermott is now?"

She shook her head.

Nomura butted in. "Were you and the deceased romantically involved?"

"We dated for a long time but had broken up six months ago."

Jacobs pulled a photograph. "Do you know this boy?"

"Of course. That's Kyle. Deke's...cousin."

"Do you know where he is?" Nomura asked.

Kristy shook her head. "Is he in trouble?"

"We'd like to talk to him," Jacobs said.

"He was at the Skunk Train the night Declan Kelly died."

There was little to infer from Nomura's tone. The internet article Kristy read glossed over the particulars. But nothing good ever happened at the Skunk Train.

"We have reason to believe—" Jacobs began.

"That your ex-boyfriend was in the middle of a drug deal with James McDermott, and that Kyle was there." Nomura paused for a reaction. "Three people died."

"It's okay, Miss Miller," Jacobs said. "Right now we're just concerned with finding the boy. Making sure he is safe. Want to talk to him, that's all."

"I don't know what to tell you. I'm worried about him too."

"Anything you can tell us about him?" Nomura asked. "Was he, well, you know how a lot of these kids walk around up here like they're gangbangers—"

"Kyle? Oh, God, no. He's a regular boy. Lonelier than most, I suppose. Angrier. But not 'gangbanger' angry. Sullen. But he's sweet, has a good heart. Is a little…misguided. He hasn't had an easy life. He lost his mother at a young age. Father's not in the picture."

"What kind of things did he do?"

"Moped. Brooded." Kristy tried to smile. "He's a very moody boy. Typical teenager." Kristy said it, but she didn't mean it. Kyle wasn't typical.

"How about any friends?"

"Have you talked to Ronnie Salk?"

"This afternoon," Jacobs said. "He was very helpful. Told us Kyle phoned from San Francisco."

"San Francisco?"

"He was there yesterday," Nomura said. "But we need to figure out where he is *now*."

Kristy knew he would try to find his father but didn't offer that. She liked Jacobs. He came across as polite and considerate, professional, not to mention soft of the eyes. But something about Nomura, with her pointy bird face and beady eyes, was unsettling, like she had ulterior motives in asking these questions. Jimmy's warning still buzzed in her brain.

"Why are you trying so hard to find Kyle?" Kristy said. "I'd like him brought home too, but you're making it sound like he's wanted for a crime. He's just a boy. Whatever Deke and Jimmy were mixed up in, Kyle had nothing to do with it, I promise you."

"Like we said," Jacobs replied. "Just want to talk to him." He extracted a business card and passed it along. "If you hear from him, give us a call, okay?"

After they were gone, Kristy grabbed the book reports. She left the glass and took the bottle.

The Driftwood lobby resembled a farmhouse from the eighteen hundreds. Paintings of churches perched on windswept bluffs, the American Sublime, island lighthouses guiding sailors home across the dark, stormy sea, white waves crashing over after-noon wine and fruit pairings on tables hand-carved from pieces of flotsam.

"Fill out the registration card," said the desk clerk, a grave and solemn man destined to forever work the night shift. "Did you park in our lot?"

Lizzie nodded.

"Include your make and model, too." He compressed his mouth into a hard, unpleasant line, gaze vacillating between them. "Parents joining you later?"

"Tomorrow," Lizzie said. "Dad had to work."

The desk clerk slid the key card. "Five-oh-nine. Right on the water." He checked the clock on the wall. "Kitchen is open for another hour, if you kids are hungry."

"That's okay. We're going to put our stuff in the room and grab a bite on Cannery Row. Call our folks."

When the elevator doors closed, Kyle tugged Lizzie's arm. "Why'd you tell that guy we were brother and sister?"

"Because I'm seventeen and you're fifteen."

"Sixteen."

"Not yet."

"Soon enough."

"Doesn't matter. No reason to draw suspicion, right? Last thing we want is some overzealous desk jockey thinking it's his civic duty to call the cops on a couple teen runaways having an underage sex party."

The capacious room overlooked the beach, with a view of the bay and peninsula. Quiet winds rustled the water and seals barked on the rocks. The reflections of restaurants and hotels shone off the shore. Sailboats twinkled far out to sea.

While Lizzie went into the bathroom, Kyle walked around the room, touching overstuffed pillows with anchors stitched on them, everything sailor-themed, navy blues and orange, golden-rod. He found the remote control and switched on the TV, sinking into the comfy chair. He rolled through the stations, kicking up his feet, feeling like a king.

Lizzie opened the door and pointed out the window. "You got a view like *that*, and you're watching TV?"

"Don't have it back home."

"No views?"

"No TV."

Lizzie wrinkled her nose.

"We have a television, but no cable or anything. Rabbit ears and tinfoil. I told you, we're poor. White trash, dirt poor. No computer. No cable. Just a dumpy trailer."

"You shared a mobile home with your grown cousin?"

"No, it was a house, but it wasn't much bigger than this room." Kyle turned off the TV and stood. "I'm not lying to you. We don't have shit. That's why I need that money. It's my chance to come up."

"Kyle, how come your father never helped you out?"

He pulled back.

"If he's making movies in Hollywood, you'd think he'd help

out his son."

"It's complicated. He and Deke didn't get on too well."

"But he's *your* dad."

"I don't know him, Lizzie. He came up for my mother's funeral when I was real little. I remember asking if I could live with him."

"What did he say?"

"He didn't say anything." Kyle went to the window. "Making movies takes up all his time. I'm not that great a son, either. I didn't reach out or anything. I'm sure I could've dug up a number on the school computer."

"Why didn't you?"

"Deke used to say his father and my father were the same, no good, that it was the two of us against the world. I guess I didn't try harder out of respect for Deke." It was weird to hear his voice say that, respecting Deke. Weirder still? He realized he meant it.

Lizzie grabbed his hand. "Wanna see Cannery Row? It's cool, all the shops in the old hatcheries. Let's go, I'll show you around." She pointed at his peach polo and sweats. "Maybe pick you up a pair of jeans and a tee shirt."

Kyle gazed at the backpack.

"It'll be fine. Hide it if it makes you feel better."

He stashed the bag under the bed.

Walking out the door, Lizzie pulled her cell. "I need to text Melanie. She said she was leaving work. She should be here soon."

CHAPTER TWENTY-FIVE

Lizzie enjoyed being back in Monterey, its lazy coastal-town feel, like Morrissey's "Every Day Is Like Sunday" without the radiation or nuclear fallout. The nostalgic trips with her dad, simpler times. Revisiting Cannery Row, she fought the urge to check his voicemails, but she already knew what each would say. *Take all the time you need, sweetheart. We're here for you when you're ready to talk.* It sounded nuts, but part of her wanted him to order her home. She needed a father, not a friend. She'd resist, of course, Lizzie was nothing if not headstrong, nobody could make her do anything when she dug in her heels for a fight, but, Christ, couldn't she have that right? You can't rebel against authority when authority grants your every wish.

The boulevard blinked with carnival lights, skyline spinning pinwheels, ice cream shops flashing neon, a cool breeze blowing off black water. They were holding hands. Such a silly thing. Lizzie couldn't remember the last time she'd just held hands with a boy. She'd done plenty of other things with boys but had skipped this part. The sweet part. The innocent part. First dates and flowers, candy and crushes, nervous over whether you are going to get kissed, all those parts that only exist in the movies, because you never walk along Cannery Row with a boy you like and hold hands in real life, not when you come from San Francisco, where everybody and -thing is irreverent, and sincerity gets earmarked an easy target.

They walked to the end of the pier and watched the boats

bob in the harbor. Lizzie couldn't stop smiling.

"What are you so happy about?"

Lizzie blushed, caught daydreaming.

Kyle pulled the pack of cigarettes they'd bought, cupping his hands and lighting one.

She plucked the lit cigarette from his hands and spun around, leaning on the pier railing. "You know why I got on the highway with you? Why I didn't drop you off at the bus station?"

He shook his head.

"My father got arrested yesterday."

"What for?"

"Police said he embezzled from his foundation. It's a charity for teen runaways. But it's huge. More like a business. A corporation. My father is brilliant. He's taught at Berkeley, Stanford. Growing up, I was convinced he could do anything he wanted. He's *too* smart, *too* good." She looked over. "That doesn't make sense, does it?"

Kyle didn't say anything.

"In a way I hope it is true. I hope he did take the money. Because then it'll mean he's actually human. Someone who can fail because he gets jealous or greedy like the rest of us. I feel like there's been a noose around my neck my whole life. It's a lot of pressure being his daughter."

Kyle lit another cigarette for himself, gazing out at sea. "I'd think having all that money would make everything great all the time."

"You have a bunch of money now. Feel any different?"

"Good point." He stopped, forehead creased with concern.

"What is it?"

"How did the guy at the impound yard know to call Melanie?"

"Huh?"

"In the car, you said Melanie told you she had your credit card because the guy at the impound called her."

"So?"

"So how would he know to call her? We didn't leave any

contact information. Melanie didn't say a word to the guy. How would he know who she was?"

Fuck.

Slinking along the carpeted hallway, Kyle wasn't sure what he was looking for; it all felt so unbelievable, these spy games. He reminded himself he was just a kid from Dormundt. Still his pulse raced. He'd made Lizzie wait around the corner by the ice machine, just in case...In case, what? Jimmy? He wasn't scared of Jimmy. It was the other stuff he hadn't told Lizzie about, the parts he didn't want to believe himself, that Deke's fears were justified. Of course the pot belonged to someone else, the money too. Until now, like the other parts of his life he didn't like, Kyle had been able to push the thought aside, tuck it out of sight, ignore it—he wanted that money. Were pissed-off redneck dealers aiming to gun him down? The mere suggestion made him want to laugh. Except his gut knotted too severe to find it funny.

At the door, Kyle bent to a knee, looking for shadows moving across the floor. He pulled the key card and swiped it. The light blinked green. Kyle pushed the door, peering inside. No noise but waves smashing against rocks. Kyle checked under the bed. There it was, like he'd left it. What an idiot. He'd worried Lizzie over nothing and ruined a nice moment on the pier. He heard her step into the room.

"Sorry," he said, sliding the backpack out and getting up. "It's still—"

Jimmy stood in the doorway behind Lizzie and Melanie. He stepped in and closed the door with his gun hand, pushing Lizzie and Melanie forward with the other. Then he strode to Kyle.

"You know the headache you've caused me, you little shit?" He smacked Kyle upside the head with the gun, producing an instant goose egg and making his ears ring. "That's for siccing the cops on me this afternoon."

"Leave him alone!"

Jimmy pointed at a chair. "Sit down."

Kyle sat and rubbed the side of his throbbing head.

Jimmy flipped the backpack on the bed, unzipping it. He pushed the bills around, as if he could count on sight, then sealed it shut. He tucked the gun in the back of his jeans and sat on the bed, facing Kyle, lips painted between snarl and sneer. He pulled the gun again and pointed it at Kyle.

"Knock it off," Lizzie said.

"Hey, Clyde. Wanna tell Bonnie to shut the fuck up?"

"Don't talk to her like that."

Jimmy shook his head with mock admiration. "Well look who went and got himself a pair of big boy balls."

"Sorry," Melanie whispered.

"I'm sure."

"Don't blame me! I told you not to get involved with this shit!"

"Knock it off, both of you." Jimmy spun around, catching Lizzie's death stare. "Give her a break. Not like I gave her any choice."

Jimmy went back to waggling his gun at Kyle, who sat perched on the edge of his seat. "What are you going to do about it?"

"Try me," Kyle said, narrowing his eyes.

"Okay." Jimmy tucked the gun behind his pants and pointed at his chin. "Go ahead, you little shit. I'll give you one shot, free and clear. Make it count."

"Leave him alone!"

"I heard you the first time, girlie. Now shut it. This is between me and Kyle." Jimmy leaned forward, holding his hands up. "One shot. Don't fuck it up like you do everything else."

Kyle wound and launched, threw the best goddamn punch of his life, connecting solid on Jimmy's chin. Jimmy's head snapped back, and for the briefest moment, Kyle swelled that he'd manned up. Then Jimmy opened his eyes, readjusted his jaw. He spat a gob of blood on the carpet and began making a buzzing sound, swatting a hand. "You hear that? I think there's a fly in here."

Then, without standing from the bed, he socked Kyle in the gut, dropping him to his knees. Kyle sucked wind, struggling to breathe.

The phone rang.

Everyone looked at each other.

Jimmy pulled the gun and aimed it at Kyle. "Quit being a pussy." When Kyle didn't move, he swung the gun at Lizzie. "Don't fuck around, you hear me? Answer it."

The phone kept ringing, Kyle slow to stir.

"Answer the fucking phone before they send someone up here!"

Kyle staggered to his feet and plucked the receiver, held it to his ear.

"This the front desk. I want to remind you kids this isn't a party house."

"Huh?"

"Two more friends of yours just arrived and asked for your room number—"

"I know. They're here—"

"I'm talking about the *other* two I just sent up."

"What other two? Nobody else knows we're here—"

Jimmy snatched the phone and slammed it down.

"The hell?"

Jimmy grabbed him by the scruff of his neck, throwing him past the two girls, hoisting the backpack under his arm, hurrying them from the room.

"What are you doing?"

Jimmy cracked the door, checking down the corridor, then turned back. "Stairs. All of you. Now!"

Kyle ripped himself free from Jimmy's grip.

"Hey, dickwad," Jimmy said. "I'm saving your ass."

"Who's down there?" Lizzie asked.

"Nobody you want to meet, trust me. Go!" Jimmy pushed

them all in the hallway and everyone ran to the exit.

Inside the stairwell, Jimmy held a finger to his mouth and stared over the railing, then waved everyone in, putting himself in front, craning over his shoulder. "Just like in school, kiddies," he said. "Single file. We get outside, you stick close to me, understand?"

Footsteps echoed off metal rungs, reverberating up the shaft, Kyle bringing up the rear. At the second-floor landing, the door swung open, and a dark hand snared him by his shirt collar, lifting him off his feet and spinning him around. Kyle's head smacked off the top step. The girls screamed. An arm wrapped around his throat, dragging him up the well. Kyle clutched and clawed for release, trying to see a face. He couldn't make out much except that the man was Mexican.

Jimmy drove up the steps, darting past, delivering three quick punches, lightning fast, like a rabbit, to the man's kidneys. The Mexican let go of Kyle and pulled his gun, firing an errant shot, which boomed like a cannon blast in the enclosed space. Cupping his ears, Kyle craned his neck as Jimmy slammed the man's head against the railing. The Mexican dropped to the ground, leaving behind a big red splotch on the bannister.

Jimmy picked up Kyle, supporting him down the stairs and guiding everyone into the salty ocean night.

CHAPTER TWENTY-SIX

Local police milled getting statements, families huddled in bathrobes, Mom and Dad clutching Junior and Sis extra tight, suburbanites from Walnut Creek and Fresno who'd expected a quaint getaway before finding themselves as extras in the opening sequence of a *CSI* episode. Carter ran a finger down the Driftwood registry, found Kyle and Lizzie's names. He glanced at Banks, who returned an unspoken understanding. Move fast before Monterey brass showed up.

Pushing through the crowd, they located the hotel's night clerk, a balding man in his thirties with a sweaty upper lip.

They flashed their badges long enough for him to see they were cops but not long enough to read names.

"Can you tell us what happened?" Carter asked.

"People kept showing up. I, I rang the room. This isn't a party house." The jittery clerk pointed toward the stairs, whispering. "Gunshots. There's…blood…up there."

"No body?"

He swiveled his head.

"Let's take a look," Carter said, peering over his shoulder as a pair of unmarked cars pulled curbside.

At the second-floor landing, they stopped at the big bloodstain on the handrail.

"Not from a gunshot," Banks said, inspecting the area.

Carter scoured the well, fixating on the hole above the doorframe. "There's the bullet."

Banks bent down, his line of sight following the steps to the basement. "Where's that lead?" he asked the clerk.

"The garbage bins and beach." The clerk gnawed his cuticles, before pulling his long, bony fingers through fine hair, threatening the few weak strands that remained.

"Street access?"

The clerk nodded.

"Thanks for your help. Go upstairs. Someone will be along soon to get an official statement."

The clerk scampered away, and Carter and Banks exited out back, into the beachside alley. Carter lit a cigarette, pinching his nose, low tide overrun with the stench of dead fish.

"Mexicans?" Banks said.

"Who the fuck else?"

"So McDermott and the girl crash the party. They're up in the room when the Mexicans show. Night jockey calls, tips them off—"

"McDermott and the other three run down the stairs, get ambushed—"

"There's a quick fight, someone's skull gets cracked open—"

"Wasn't one of ours. Mexicans aren't leaving a job undone."

"So you think McDermott got the better of it?"

"My guess."

"Tough fucker. Where's that leave us?" Banks asked.

Carter flicked his cigarette into a heap of wet trash bags. "Screwed."

"We have the plates. And we got the girl's cell number."

"First thing McDermott does now is ditch that truck. Right after he throws everyone's cells out the window. This guy isn't as dumb as he looks."

Behind the wheel of the hot-wired '94 Civic, hand gripping the 9mm in his lap, Jimmy scanned the side and rearview mirrors. He had joy-ridden these cars so many times as a teen he could take apart the engine and put it back together in his sleep.

As soon as they were out of harm's way, first thing Jimmy did was collect cells and purses. The purses he stashed with the cash in the trunk. He smashed the cells. They could triangulate that shit. New ride or not, they needed to ditch the road and get off the grid.

"Where are you taking us?" Lizzie asked from the back.

"Let us go," Melanie pleaded.

"Yeah, hon, no can do."

"Why not?"

"For one, you'll be killed."

"What do you care?" Kyle said from the passenger seat.

"Your cousin was my best friend. Just because you treated him like shit while he was alive, I'm not going to disgrace his memory and leave you to get whacked."

"Okay, Tony Soprano."

"Laugh it up. You know who was choking the shit out of you back there?" Jimmy caught Lizzie's eye in the rearview. "Not so fun now, is it, sweetheart?" He backhanded Kyle's shoulder. "You got any smokes?"

Kyle passed him one.

"That," Jimmy said through a deep inhale, "was the Mexican mafia. The *cartel*." Jimmy emphasized the Spanish, rolling the r and l.

"Yeah, right."

"Where do you think your cousin and me got the weed from?"

"Your dealer."

"And who supplied him, dumbass? We found Bodhi and his two wives, hogtied." Jimmy held out two fingers pointed like a barrel, cocked his thumb like a hammer. "Back of the head. Execution style."

Melanie whimpered.

"Yeah," Jimmy said, "it was all fun and games when you three were dicking around with my money, playing Spy Kids.

Now it's for real, fuckos."

"You got the money," Kyle said. "They're after you. Not us."

"You were at the Skunk Train."

"We weren't," Melanie cried. "Let Lizzie and me go."

"I'm doing you a favor, honey. You don't know who you're dealing with. We ain't just talking the mob and hick dope dealers." He thumbed toward the trunk. "Where you think that money came from? That's dirty cop money."

"How do you know?" Kyle said.

"Because the police aren't running a sting in bumfuck Dormundt. And if they *were*, I'd be in jail by now. They'd have every highway road-blocked from here to Canada, Nevada and Mexico. You can't shoot at cops and drive off. No, that was some funky shit back at the Skunk Train." Jimmy's voice trailed off in a sing-song as he weaved past a tractor trailer. "My guess? Some good ol' boys were trying to make a quick buck."

"Where would cops in Dormundt get that much money?"

"Bust. Evidence room. A dealer. Savings. Who knows? But they were trying to pull a fast one. Until those bikers showed up." Jimmy turned to Kyle. "But you wouldn't know anything about that, would you?"

"Bullshit." Kyle folded his arms and stared out the window.

"Either way, you're coming with me."

"What if we don't *want* to come with you?"

"Too fucking bad."

Melanie began sobbing.

"Everyone relax, okay? No one is getting abducted. If the Mexicans are looking for us in Monterey, I can't very well kick you to the curb, can I? And if the Mexicans found you there, so can those crooked cops. We're going to get somewhere safe, far away, together, and then y'all can be on your merry way." He turned to Kyle. "You wanted to see your dad, right?"

"Yeah. So?"

"We go to L.A. Place is so big, couple kids kicking it on a

street corner won't stand out as much. Don't be dumb enough to register with your own name this time."

"What about us?" Melanie asked, fighting back the tears.

"I don't give a shit what you do." Jimmy craned his head out the window, checking signs, before veering off the exit. "Call Mommy and Daddy to pick you up."

"We can't. You trashed our phones."

"I'll buy you a calling card." Jimmy pulled into a roadside gas station, killing the engine. He jammed the keys in his jeans pocket and climbed out, poking his head through the window. "Now nobody be stupid. I'll be right over there." He pointed fifteen yards away at the plexiglass attendant box.

After he was gone, Kyle turned and stared at Lizzie, who mouthed a "no."

"We should run," Melanie said.

"Where?" asked Lizzie. "It's midnight, we're in the middle of nowhere. No cells. No money. How far you think we're getting?"

"We could flag down a cop?"

Lizzie didn't answer her, instead focusing on Kyle. "You think he's telling the truth? About the dirty cops and Mexicans?"

"I don't know. Maybe."

"How bad was that shootout up there?"

"Bad."

"You could've told me that."

"I did."

"No, you glossed over that part. You made it seem like no big deal and that you were in the clear."

"I never said that!"

"Settle down, Romeo," Jimmy said, sliding back in the driver's seat. "The Greyhound station is fifteen miles. Salinas. Gonna catch the midnight express. Just pulled out of San Francisco. Should be passing through soon. A lot safer than riding in a hot car."

"I don't want to ride on a fucking bus."

"Too fucking bad, *Kyle*. We ain't driving a stolen car to L.A. They don't check IDs on a Greyhound." Jimmy pulled out of the station, zipping back onto the desolate freeway. "Try and show some gratitude, you little shit. I'm the only thing keeping you alive right now."

CHAPTER TWENTY-SEVEN

A helicopter swooped low, hovering in a pre-dawn sky the color of bruised eggplant, its high-powered beams trained through tenement windows, into the back seats of grounded cars and gutted vans, up alleyways crawling with rodents and over vagabonds passed out in their own sick. Old newspapers swirled in the blade winds below, like some post-apocalyptic tumbleweed. All around them, nomads mumbled and shuffled their feet, zombied directionless, basketcases with blistered lips and peeper-frog eyes, speaking in tongues, palsied hands outstretched, begging for mercy that wasn't coming.

Welcome to the City of Angels.

They huddled around Jimmy as he delivered them through the burning barrels of Skid Row. Despite the raw hour, police and ambulance sirens wailed from every direction, car alarms sounding in the distance.

For as much as they all hated Jimmy, no one was leaving his side.

Jimmy looked over his shoulder, catching their eyes. "Try not to act so scared. I won't let anything happen to you, okay?"

"What is this place?" Lizzie asked.

"I'm pretty sure this is hell, baby."

Rounding a corner, they entered Tent City, endless rows of blue tarps stretched over rebar skeletons. Like a war-torn outpost, the scarred remains of a pirate battlefield, the cardboard shantytown overrun with bramble weeds, shopping carts, and discarded syringes. Rats the size of cats gnawed on tiny bones.

They pushed ahead toward downtown, past a tall, decrepit building wrapped in scaffolding, blinking lights proclaiming it the Million Dollar Hotel, as cabs and buses started to crawl, the lowlife workweek waking up.

Jimmy checked street signs, stopped at a stoop. Inside a dirty window: "Weekly Rents Available."

"We're not staying here," Melanie said.

"I have business around the corner in a few hours."

A man with a ragged beard approached, tugging at Jimmy's sleeve, paper cup in hand. "Anything? Anything?"

"Get out of my face," Jimmy said, giving him a shove. "Get a fucking job."

"Jesus will remember that," the man mumbled, limping across the street like a kicked dog.

Jimmy rang the bell and the buzzer sounded. He piled everyone in, pulling the metal grate closed.

"Wait here."

Like anyone thought of moving.

A few minutes later Jimmy waved them upstairs to the lobby, and they all crammed through the accordion gate into the rickety elevator and up to the third floor. At a scarred red door, Jimmy pushed the key into the lock.

"Welcome home."

The single room sported a bed, chair, and rust-stained sink, grimy walls flecked with speckled red. The room stank like urine, antiseptic, and cigarette smoke.

"Where's the bathroom?" Melanie asked.

"The sink." Jimmy gestured out the door. "Down the hall."

"I'll hold it."

"What are we doing here?" Lizzie asked.

"I don't know about you, but I need some sleep. I didn't get any on the bus." Jimmy walked to the window. The limited view overlooked the alley, inch-thick pigeon excrement caked on the fire escape. He smacked the underside of the sill with his palm. Painted shut.

"All that money, you couldn't get us a nicer place?" Kyle asked. "Maybe *two* rooms?"

"Yeah, I'm going to get you guys your own room." Jimmy slid the chair in front of the door. "I know a guy in this neighborhood. Worked out a deal to clean this money."

"Who?" Kyle said.

"None of your fucking business." Jimmy dropped in the chair, propping his feet on the backpack, which now also contained the girls' purses, hand resting on the grip of the gun tucked in his waistband. "Might as well take a load off. And don't try anything. I'm a light sleeper." He pointed at the shaving kit Kyle clutched to his chest. "What's in there?"

"None of *your* business."

Jimmy shook him off, addressing all three. "I promise, when I get up and meet my guy, you're free to go. I'll even buy the bus ticket back home."

"You're a helluva guy," Kyle said.

Jimmy tipped his imaginary cap.

"Why can't we go now?"

"Because I said so. I don't need one of you little shits flagging down a cop or calling Mommy and Daddy before I have *my* money. Until then, shitbirds, rest up." Jimmy shut his eyes.

Melanie, Lizzie, and Kyle all looked at each other.

"I'm not getting in the same bed as him," Melanie said.

"Then sleep on the floor."

Lizzie and Kyle crawled under the covers. She pulled his arm over her, curling into him.

Despite the bloody wails from ground zero, it only took a few moments before everyone had fallen sleep.

Banks sat down in the booth as the waitress finished pouring Carter a cup of coffee.

"Thought you didn't touch the stuff?"

Carter held up a hand and she pulled back the pot. "Bad habits gotta start sometime. Anything?"

"Got a hit."

"Where?"

"Stolen Civic, about four blocks from the Driftwood."

"Must've switched cars three times by now." Carter dumped a mound of sugar into his mug, clanking the spoon against clay walls.

"Not driving a car anymore. Civic owner forgot his cell in the console. Had an app to track it. Greyhound station in Salinas."

"Anyone recognize our guys?"

Banks beamed. "Rough-looking shit-kicker approximately thirty years old, three teenagers, two girls and a boy. Only luggage: a big brown backpack. Boarded the one-forty."

"Headed?"

"Downtown L.A."

"East Seventh. Skid Row."

Banks stared.

"Old man was a merchant marine." Carter slurped his coffee, gumming out his tongue and pinching his face. "How's anyone drink this shit? Tastes like cat ass."

CHAPTER TWENTY-EIGHT

"Fucking bitch!"

Kyle jolted awake. Bright yellow sunshine flooded through the open window. His arm was still curled around Lizzie. Even though he couldn't see her eyes, he knew she wasn't sleeping.

Jimmy slapped the backpack on the bed, face burning red. He tore it open but calmed down once he fanned through the cash. "She just took her purse." He shook his head in disbelief, exhaling. "Fucking dumb bitch."

Kyle rubbed the sleep from his eyes and rolled toward the nightstand, snagging the pack of cigarettes and lighting one with a match.

Jimmy was still shaking his head. "Toss me those." Then to Lizzie: "You sure can pick them."

Lizzie didn't respond. Kyle followed her gaze to the open window leading to the fire escape.

"She must've pried it open," Lizzie whispered. "She left us here."

"She also left your purse," Jimmy said, tossing the handbag at Lizzie's feet.

"What now?" asked Kyle.

"Now," Jimmy said, cigarette dangling, shirt unbuttoned all the way to his taut country boy gut, "I got a deal to make."

"What about us?"

"You—ain't my problem no more." Jimmy swung the backpack over his shoulder.

"What the fuck are we supposed to do?"

"I don't give a shit."

"We don't have any money."

"I'm sure your girlfriend's got plenty of credit cards in that purse—she's got a rich mommy and daddy who are a phone call away."

Kyle stood, shoulders squared, chin up. "That was Deke's money too."

"And Deke's dead. Your point?"

Kyle didn't back down. Wiry as Jimmy was, he still had Kyle by at least forty pounds, and he seemed to have muscles in all the right places, tight cords of sinew and wrought ligament. And he was mean as a snake caught in a well. But Kyle wasn't letting him walk out without getting paid.

Jimmy spat a laugh. He unzipped the backpack, then counted out ten one-hundred-dollar bills, tossing them on the mattress.

"That ain't for you," he said. "That's for your cousin. You understand? I don't owe *you* anything."

"There's at least a hundred grand in there—"

"Don't push it. Or I'll take it back."

Kyle grabbed a hundred, and Jimmy clasped his wrist. "How about a fucking thank you?"

"Gee, thanks, Jimmy."

Jimmy threw his wrist down.

Lizzie remained on the bed, hands around knees, head down, silent.

"Hey," Jimmy called to her.

She peered up.

"I don't know you, but do yourself a favor, sweetheart. Go home." He gestured at Kyle. "This one here ain't worth your time of day. Kid's a fuck-up. Been that way his whole life. I tried setting his cousin straight, but he wouldn't listen. Everyone this little shit knows, from his mother to his father to his cousin, ends up six feet under or running away. Do the math."

"You're right," Lizzie said. "You don't know me."

Jimmy stubbed the cigarette out on the arm of the chair. He went to tuck the pack away but instead tossed it to Kyle. "What the fuck do I care what you two do? The room's paid for till noon. Have some fun."

He secured the backpack and opened the door.

The gunshot was muffled by a suppressor, but at point-blank range, a good chunk of Jimmy's head still blew off. Blood sprayed the walls and tiny globs of purple brain rained down on the bed sheets.

Jimmy's body remained standing impossibly still a moment. Then it dropped to the floor with a lifeless thud.

The first man, the bigger of the two, nudged Jimmy's corpse aside with the toe of his boot as if it were roadkill. The second man, blockier and stouter, ambled in behind him and pulled the door shut.

He dropped to a knee and pried the strap from Jimmy's dead hands. He alternated between Kyle and Lizzie. "Don't look so scared. We're cops."

The other man flapped open a wallet, shiny silver badge displayed. "Carter," he said. "That's Banks."

Carter bent forward and scooped the hundreds off the bed.

"That's mine."

"We can sort it out later, Kyle," Carter said, pocketing the cash before dropping into the seat that had been occupied by the dead man. He slipped off his coat, exposing the gun in his shoulder holster.

Banks went to the window, running fingers over the peeled edges. "This was painted shut. Someone pried it open."

"Nothing to worry about." Carter turned to Lizzie. "You two gave us quite the runaround." He waited for her to respond. When she didn't, he leaned over and picked up her purse. He sifted through the items inside, extracting her driver's license. "Elizabeth A. Decker. Elizabeth Street. San Francisco." He smirked. "Elizabeth on Elizabeth Street. That's funny."

"Elizabeth is my mother's name."

"Even funnier."

"How'd you find us?" Kyle asked.

"You pissed off the wrong hobo."

"So, hotshot, want to tell us what happened at the Skunk Train."

Kyle narrowed his eyes.

"We can do this here. Or we can haul you both in. However you want it."

Banks pointed a stubby finger at Lizzie. "Don't think a nice family like the Deckers want their daughter mixed up with the law, do you?"

"I don't know anything," Kyle said.

Banks extracted a pair of handcuffs, twirling it around his finger like a miniature hula-hoop.

"What do you want to know?"

"What'd you see?"

"Nothing."

"Nothing?"

"Does it look like I'm a drug dealer? I'm a sophomore in high school."

Banks tapped the backpack on the bed. "Looks like a helluva education to me."

"That…just happened."

"You just *happened* to be at the Skunk Train?"

"My cousin brought me there. He was worried someone was going to come looking for the pot."

"No shit, numb-nuts."

"But he didn't tell me who. He stuck me in the room. Then he and Jimmy worked out a deal."

"Who was the buyer?"

"How should I know?"

"Didn't get a good look at the men?"

Kyle shook his head.

Carter, who had been leaning back in the chair, let the front legs fall. He backhanded Banks' arm. "Come on. He doesn't know anything."

"Jimmy was the one you should've asked."

Carter hopped up and stepped to Kyle. "What Jimmy tell you?"

"Nothing. He was paranoid, talking out his ass. Had this whole conspiracy with cops and the mob."

Carter and Banks swapped a long look, before Banks pointed at the shaving kit on the nightstand. "What's in there?"

"Nothing. It's...private."

Banks grabbed the kit and extracted a stack of folded papers. "What's this?"

"Letters from my father."

"Letters?"

"Yeah, letters."

"Anything else in there?" Carter asked Banks.

Banks sifted around, plucking a picture, holding it up.

"That's all?" Carter said. "Let him have it." He curled his fingers. "Okay, you two lovebirds."

"Where are you taking us? We didn't do anything."

"I think you did plenty, Kyle." Banks took Lizzie by the arm. "What do we do with him?" Banks asked, pointing down at Jimmy's body.

"Leave him for the maids."

They pushed Kyle and Lizzie into the musty hall. Kyle tried to get Lizzie's attention, but she stared straight ahead. She hadn't said much since Carter and Banks barged in. Who could blame her? She'd just watched a man murdered in cold blood. Kyle wanted two minutes alone with her, to tell her how sorry he was and promise he'd get her out of this. He felt the little Swiss army knife in his back pocket, which he'd held onto while he slept. He clutched it for protection, but doubted that dull, old thing could pierce apple skin. He craved a lethal weapon. He had to do something, but what? Step on the big guy's toe and sprint into the L.A. sun, holding hands like a pair of teen runaways? This wasn't the movies.

* * *

No doors cracked open, no inquisitive eyes peered out from the dark. A gunshot was nothing new around here. Lizzie accepted no cavalry was coming to their rescue.

The bright white daylight drew a hand to her face. No one spoke as the cops directed them down the garbage-strewn alley, past overflowing green bins butted against brown brick. Feral cats screeched in secluded corners.

At the mouth of the alley, a maroon car waited, not even a removable siren on its hood, just a regular sedan.

"They're going to kill us," Lizzie whispered.

"They can't kill us. They're cops."

"Tell that to your buddy, Jimmy."

"Where are you taking us?" Kyle asked, and Banks yawned.

"Get in." Carter opened the back door, shoving them inside. Banks unlocked the trunk and tossed in the backpack and purse, slamming the trunk shut. Outside the car, Carter said something to his partner but Lizzie couldn't hear what.

She ran her eyes up the sides of tall tenements, around the busy city streets teeming with people. Couldn't she bang on the glass? Scream for help? There had to be at least *one* person who'd do the right thing. Watching each indifferent face pass by, Lizzie knew they'd be dead before anyone even glanced their way.

The two cops climbed up front. Banks draped his arm holding the gun over the passenger headrest. "Relax and you'll both be home, right as rain, real soon."

The violent impact came from the driver's side, metal crumpling like a stepped-on soda can, windshield shattering, tiny diamonds splashing on the asphalt. Lizzie was thrown into Kyle, knocking him to the floor. The recoil snapped her head back against the window so hard she saw stars.

Lizzie reached out for Kyle, who lay on the floor fumbling. She turned and saw the man approach. Dark skin with dark glasses, he wore the suit like he was on his way to the office before getting sidetracked. At the driver's side window, Carter's head slumped on his chest. The Mexican fired three quick shots into his gut. Carter fell forward, landing on the horn, before the man leaned in and yanked him off. Banks' skull was stuck halfway out the broken window, impaled on jags of glass, his empty hands positioned on the dash, as if already locked in rigor mortis. The Mexican fired three more shots, jolting the dead man's jelly center like a sow stuck with an electric prod.

The Mexican looked back at Lizzie, without expression. He had a bandage on his forehead. Lizzie tugged on Kyle's shirt, pulling him up. The Mexican's stare remained fixed as he dipped a hand along the interior runner and popped the trunk. Lizzie heard footsteps stop behind them. Then another click, and the doors unlocked. The Mexican with the bandage on his head stood at the window, nodded once toward the door. Lizzie opened it, took Kyle by the hand, and together they ran, fleeing through the alley.

They'd run ten twisted city blocks before Lizzie couldn't run anymore. She bent over, hands on her knees, panting.

Los Angeles flared around them like an endless strip mall of the cheap and uninspired. Lean, angry young men swilled from paper bags on apartment stoops; thick women shuffled batfaced broods in and out of *supermercados*.

Kyle came up beside Lizzie. "You okay?"

"They have my purse."

"I dropped my shaving kit too. It's all right."

"No, it's not." Lizzie pointed into the air, which carried the slicing sounds of emergency sirens. "You lost a couple pictures. I lost my ID. My credit cards. My money."

"I have money." Kyle plucked the hundred he'd managed to pocket, holding it up.

"Put that away. Do you even know where we are?"

"I know where we are. I'm not stupid."

"How long you think a hundred dollars is going to last us

down here?"

"No one says you have to stay. You can go home."

"No, I can't! Didn't you hear me? All my personal information is in the trunk of a car with two dead cops, and I'm on the run with someone wanted for a shootout with police!"

"Aren't you being dramatic?"

"Sorry. I forgot about the dead redneck in the hotel room." Kyle stood straight and scanned the streets. "Where are we?"

"How should I know?"

"You blame me for all this."

"Who else is there to blame? You stole drugs and money—"

"I told you, I didn't *steal* anything."

"No, your cousin did. You swore to me at the impound that the money was yours—"

"No. I said I had every bit as much right to it as Jimmy did."

"Listen to yourself. Do you take *any* responsibility?"

"Yeah, Lizzie, I do. I feel like shit that Deke is dead. I feel terrible that you're mixed up in all this. How was I supposed to know a couple dirty cops were going to try to kidnap us or that the Mexican mob would be on our tail?"

"What do you think happens when you steal people's money?"

"I didn't *steal* anything!"

"Someone did! You don't stumble onto giant bags stuffed with narcotics and think no one's going to miss them."

"You don't know what it's like up there. Everyone has a grow house or room or field to harvest. I didn't know where Deke and Jimmy pinched that haul from, but it's not *that* weird they'd have it. My cousin wasn't a thief."

"Just a drug dealer."

"Pot. Not the same thing. And you smoke. Where do you think it comes from? Someone's growing it. Someone has to sell it—"

"Stop," Lizzie said. "I'm tired of it. You're fifteen and think you have everything figured out."

"Like you're so much older."

"No. I'm not. And I don't have *any*thing figured out. In fact, I've never felt so confused my entire life. It's not like everything was great, but it wasn't this screwed up until you came along. Maybe Jimmy was right about you." Lizzie stopped herself. "I'm sorry. I shouldn't have said that." She blew out a gust and cleared the sweaty hair from her eyes. "What do we do now?"

"You should call your parents."

"I told you I can't do that."

"Well, I'm going to find my father."

"I thought you said you lost the address."

"I did. But I remember the neighborhood that woman wrote down."

"What woman?"

"The one living in my uncle's old apartment in San Francisco. The street was Portal or Port? One thousand and something. Echo Park."

Lizzie threw her hands up and began walking away. She stopped and turned around. "You coming or not?"

They started down the street, far apart at first, gradually drifting nearer.

When they were close enough to touch, Kyle looked over. "By the way, you can stop saying I'm fifteen. Today's my birthday."

CHAPTER TWENTY-NINE

It had taken Kyle a long time to decide on the exact street name. He asked strangers, scoured bus stop maps. He settled on Portia. He was pretty sure that was it. They walked up Cesar Chavez and caught the Sunset Boulevard line to Echo Park. The trip depressed him, bus jammed with Mexican women hauling baskets of laundry as sugar-fueled kids raced up and down the aisle. There hadn't been anywhere to sit with Lizzie. He wanted to talk to her, try to repair some of the damage. He'd gotten defensive in the alleyway and regretted the way he'd acted. He knew he'd screwed up. The past few days he'd done nothing but. Instead of possible atonement he got stuck next to an old man who smelled like fish. It wasn't the greatest time to be alone with his thoughts. Deke's death and Jimmy's constant insults would've been tough enough without the new asshole Lizzie had ripped him. But she was right. When he found the money, he should've gone to the police. Who can think straight in the middle of a shit storm like that? After what he'd witnessed? Anyone would've been rattled. The more Kyle fixated on how lost he felt, the less he could trace a crooked road back to one wrong turn. His life had been off course for a while. He'd thought money would fix the problem. Like all he needed was to run away and start over. He knew now it wouldn't matter if he scored a golden chariot. He'd never be able to outrun himself.

The flats of Los Angeles flipped past the big bus windows like a deck of pale playing cards. Up north, purple mountains and green valleys livened the landscape, the scenery rich, lush, robust. Down here, the world felt washed out, as if relentless sunshine had bleached all the color. Faded pavement. Blanched blue skies. Windswept fields, locked behind chain-link fences, absorbed into the blinding horizon. The endless ride reminded Kyle he was a helluva lot closer to the border than he was his home.

They exited at Portia Street, on the fourteen-hundred block, in front of a hole-in-the-wall bar called Little Joy. The bus coughed a cloud of exhaust and slogged off. Kyle surveyed the squalid neighborhood. Knocking on every door would take all day. A red-faced Hispanic stumbled out of the bar. Not even noon and already sloshed.

"You sure this is the street?"

"Pretty sure. It was a thousand-something. And there was a half. Twelve-forty-one-and-a-half maybe?"

"Is there *any*thing you know about your uncle?"

"I know he drinks. A lot."

Lizzie motioned at the sign for Little Joy. "Good a place as any to get started." Lizzie took a step toward the red-faced drunk, who had stopped on the sidewalk to spit out something chunky and alien. "Do you know—" She turned to Kyle. "What's your uncle's name?"

"Joe Kelly."

"You know a Joe Kelly? Lives on this street?"

The man batted a hand and waved her off, then proceeded to throw up.

Lizzie jumped back. "Disgusting."

The drunken Hispanic wiped a string of drool from his mouth, moving toward her. "What you say, bitch?"

Kyle sprung past, wedging between them, and shoved the man, who ass-planted in his own puke. Like a boxer whose bell has been rung, the drunkard staggered to his feet and gazed around glassy-eyed, trying to figure out where he was, before zigzagging down Sunset.

"Look at you," Lizzie said, smiling.

Kyle turned away so she wouldn't catch him turn red.

The bartender stepped outside, wiping his hands on a filthy rag. "You kids can't be hanging outside a bar."

"What do you care?" Kyle said.

"When you're assaulting my customers, I care." He looked them both over. "Don't you have school or something?"

"Do you know Joe Kelly?"

The bartender narrowed his eyes. "Why?"

"Do you know where he lives? He's my uncle."

"Sucks to be you." He seemed to lighten up. "I eighty-sixed his ass last month. Mutherfucker doesn't like to pay his tab." He pointed several apartments down. "You're practically standing on his front lawn. Fourteen-twenty-one-and-a-half. Cottage around back. The red one there. Lives with his girlfriend. Real piece of work."

"Thanks."

"No problem. When you see him, tell him Marlon from Little Joy says he can go fuck himself."

The dilapidated cottage stood behind the main duplex, a set of rickety stairs leading to a porch missing a plank. Kyle knocked. He could hear a baby crying inside. When no one answered, he pounded harder.

A woman came to the door, screeching baby on her hip. She looked both young and haggard at the same time. The place was as wretched as the dump on Jones Street.

"Whatever you're selling, we don't want it." She went to close the door.

Kyle stuck his foot inside the frame. "I'm looking for my uncle."

"Your uncle doesn't live here."

"Is this Joe Kelly's house?"

"First of all, it's not a house. It's an apartment. And, yes, Joe does live here, but he doesn't have any brothers or sisters, so I doubt he has any nephews."

The baby began to bawl louder.

"He does have a brother. My dad. Can I talk to him?"

"He's not here. Try the bar or OTB."

"You have to know my father. He's a director. In Hollywood."

"Sweetheart, if we had any rich, famous Hollywood relatives, you think we'd be living in this hellhole?"

"Alan. Alan Smith? That's his professional name, the one he goes by. With two e's. They're silent. Are you sure you never heard of him?"

"For the last time. No. Now please go."

The woman kicked his foot free and slammed the door.

Back on Portia, Kyle slid against a sidewall, knees up. He began plucking tiny stones and arcing them into the street. Lizzie slumped beside him.

"Sorry," she said.

Kyle fisted some pebbles, sifted the best, tossed them too.

"Kyle, you sure that was your uncle's house? That woman had a point. Who lies about having a famous relative?"

"Maybe famous was a stretch." He stopped. "I'm not lying that he's directed movies. A bunch of them. Some TV shows. Get a computer. You can look him up."

"It's more the part about how she didn't know he exists. Why wouldn't he mention a brother?"

"Maybe they had a fight. I don't know."

Lizzie didn't want to hurt his feelings any more than they already were. It was obvious what was happening. "How much do you know about your dad?"

"Not as much as I thought."

"When was the last time you saw him?"

"After my mom died. About ten years ago. I told you. He came up for the funeral. Then he left and I went to stay with Deke."

"You never arranged a visit?"

"A bunch of times. But right before I was supposed to come down—"

"Something would come up?"

"He said I could come live with him when I got older. Deke told me."

"You told that woman he goes by his stage name."

"Alan Smith."

"Spelled with two e's?"

"They're silent. So what?"

"Forget it. Never mind. I don't know shit about movies."

"No. Tell me."

Lizzie didn't want to be the one to tell him. "Alan Smithee is the pseudonym directors use when they want to distance themselves from a particular project. It's not a real name. He doesn't exist."

Kyle sprung up. "You're right. You don't know shit about movies." He headed up the sidewalk toward West Sunset.

Lizzie ran after him. "Hey, come on. Don't be like that." She went to grab his arm, but he tugged it away.

"You think I'm an idiot."

"No, I don't. I think you're a boy who wants to find his dad."

"You didn't believe me about the money either. I'm not lying about the letters. I had stacks of them in the shaving kit. But I can't show you now, can I?"

"I don't doubt you received letters from your father, and I'm sure he bragged about being a director. But after seeing that woman's house, hearing about your uncle, I think your father's lying."

"Because you're such an expert on honest fathers?"

"That's not fair."

"Why would he do that?"

Lizzie shrugged. "Who knows why fathers do what they do?"

"You can look it up on the internet, if you want," Kyle said, once more, less sure.

Lizzie stopped pressing. The expression on his face killed her. It was the look of someone who finally admitted he'd been lying to himself for years. There's no way Kyle hadn't searched the name "Alan Smithee" at some point. He didn't want to believe it. So he pretended the fantasy was real. We all do it. She took his hand, squeezed it.

"Let's get a hotel room," she said. "We could both use something to eat. We'll figure out what to do in the morning."

Following a miserable day teaching, Kristy phoned Detective Jacobs. She knew she had to tell the cops everything.

They met at a coffee shop on Laughlin in Cutting, Jacobs' idea, probably figuring it would be less unnerving than the precinct. She was glad he'd come alone. Kristy didn't trust that Nomura.

They sat at a patio table outside, the Northern California skies churning overcast and blustery. Cubicle jockeys and college students, gassing up on caffeine in between late-afternoon meetings and classes, passed by, carrying on animated conversations.

"I'm glad you called," he said.

"How much trouble is Kyle in?"

"It's not good. Two cops, detectives from Richter, were found this morning. Shot dead in their car in L.A."

"Los Angeles? You don't think Kyle had anything to do with that, do you? If you met him, you'd know how crazy that sounds—"

Jacobs held up a hand. "No one is accusing anyone of anything. These two detectives, let's say there's extenuating circumstances—but evidence places Kyle at the scene. That, coupled with the Skunk Train, makes him a person of serious interest. We're talking big time, feds. Do you know where Kyle would go in Los Angeles?"

Kristy gnawed on her bottom lip. "He thinks his father lives in Hollywood."

"Thinks? Meaning, he doesn't?"

Kristy fidgeted in her seat.

"I can't help Kyle unless I know the whole story."

"This is going to sound bad. It's going to make Deke look like an asshole. He wasn't. He loved Kyle. I think he was trying to, y'know, give him a father to be proud of, instead of the drunken piece of shit he is." Kristy paused again, working to get the words right. "It's not going to help you find Kyle any faster, trust me. I don't know where his father lives. Neither did Deke. Last he'd heard, Joe, that's his dad, had moved to Los Angeles. This was years ago. They hadn't had any contact in a very long time."

"Wait. Whose dad?"

"Kyle and Deke's."

"Brothers?"

"Half brothers. Same father. Deke was a lot older than Kyle. One of Joe Kelly's other marriages. Joe collected wives like some people do cars. Kyle never knew. He'd been so young when his mom died. Joe didn't want him around, and Deke wasn't going to let his brother go to Social Services."

Jacobs bobbed his head like he understood. "This story we've been hearing around Dormundt, from Kyle's classmates and teachers, about his dad being a famous director, Deke made that part up too?"

"I don't think Deke anticipated Kyle clinging to it so much. When he first took him in, he wanted to give Kyle something to feel good about. The boy was pretty screwed up. He's always been off. Not bad, just damaged."

"Why didn't he tell Kyle they were brothers?"

"You didn't know Deke. He had a way of doing things. Very stubborn, pigheaded. He had a strict code he lived by, and I didn't always understand why he did what he did, but that's how he did it. My guess? His plan backfired." Kristy waited a moment. "Did you know Deke owned his own house? Bought it himself. Before he was twenty. Worked his ass off to get it. It wasn't much. But it was his. Deke wasn't school smart, but he had something." Remembering him, Kristy couldn't help but smile. "None of that impressed Kyle. He preferred the superhero father fantasy. Even after Deke stopped with the letters."

"Letters?"

"At first Deke would write letters to Kyle, pretending they were from his father. How much he missed him, about the movies he was working on. Problem is, the real thing can never live up to the fantasy. Deke was ashamed of never having gone to college. He didn't even graduate high school. He got his GED, took extension courses at Community. I think he wanted to come up first and make Kyle proud of him, as weird as it sounds."

"It doesn't sound that weird." Detective Jacobs placed his hand on hers. "This has all been very helpful. We'll let Los Angeles know. It'll be easy to run Kelly's name through DMV and get his residence. We'll put someone on his place." Jacobs appeared pained. "I have to ask you something. It's not going to be easy. But I need you to be honest, okay?"

Kristy nodded.

"The picture we're getting of Kyle isn't a good one. The people we've spoken to—friends, people in town, school counselor. Kyle comes across as a loner with a loose fuse."

"What's your question?"

"Would you consider Kyle mentally ill?"

"I'm not the person to ask, Detective Jacobs. I teach grade school English. You'd have to ask a doctor."

"We did. The school psychologist seems to think so."

"Kyle is a teenage boy who needs to be loved."

"I'm looking for your opinion, that's all. Three men died at the Skunk Train. Three more have been found dead in L.A. The only person with ties to all these shootings is Kyle. When cops die, other cops get worked up, and that's when bad things happen."

"But Kyle's not the only one."

"Huh?"

"You said Kyle was the only one. That's not true. What about Jimmy? Now there's a real sociopath. I've seen him—"

"Jim McDermott's body was one of the ones found this

morning in L.A. Skid Row hotel room. Shot in the head."

Kristy covered her mouth.

"I can also tell you, one of the dead cops I mentioned was missing his gun, and that witnesses saw a boy matching Kyle's description fleeing the scene. A call goes out that he may be armed, it creates an entirely different response. Kyle also has a young woman in his company. Comes from a wealthy family in San Francisco. No one is saying she went against her will. We're still trying to determine that. But all these details added together paint an unflattering picture."

Kristy didn't know much about law enforcement, but she'd seen enough cop shows to know that "armed" was almost always followed by "dangerous." Which translated to: shoot first, forget the questions.

"I don't want you to worry," Jacobs said. "But after all you've told me, if Kyle *has* come in possession of a gun, given his already precarious mental state, I'm wondering what his reaction will be when he learns his whole life has been a lie."

CHAPTER THIRTY

Kyle said he didn't care where they went as long as it was like the SoCal in his mind, somewhere with palm trees and crashing waves, blue skies and carefree, cloudless days. They caught the bus toward Hollywood and found a cheap room at the Tropicana Motor Inn. It had one palm tree in front and a dirty green pool crawling with algae. There was a family restaurant across the road.

While Lizzie took a shower, Kyle sat on the edge of the motel bed, opening and closing his little pocketknife, running over ways to fix this problem. There was no way out for him. That was okay. People had been telling him he was no good for so long, he'd come to accept it. But he couldn't allow Lizzie to get dragged down, too. He owed her more than that.

The water cut off.

The bathroom door opened. Lizzie stood there, naked, her long brown hair curled into wet ringlets. She didn't speak, just stared at him with soulful eyes. Kyle swallowed hard and his breathing grew rapid. She made no effort to cover up, and he drank it all in. He'd never seen anything so perfect.

"Come here," she said, beckoning with a finger, and he rose and followed her instructions like an eager pup.

He stopped in front of her and could feel her heat. She lifted his shirt above his head, hooked two fingers into the belt loops of his jeans, pulling him in and kissing him softly on the mouth, pressing their bodies together.

She guided them both toward the bed, Kyle stutter-stepping backwards, head swirling with a million thoughts. He bumped against the frame, and Lizzie playfully pushed his shoulders. He fell back on the mattress.

"Happy birthday," she whispered.

Kyle woke sometime after midnight and checked to make sure she was still there and that it hadn't all been a dream. The sheet lay below her smooth, exposed shoulder, moonlight shining through the window, silhouetting her shape.

He got out of bed and lit a cigarette. Standing there, he peered out through a crack in the drapes, toward the mountains in the distance. The full moon hung white and bright, splashing down on the pool, which shimmered in the soft breeze. He'd turned a year older, but following these last few days, Kyle felt like he'd aged a dozen. He knew what he had to do.

Kyle found his jeans in the dark. After the room and dinner, he had a few bucks left.

He got dressed and opened the door, turning back to look at Lizzie, sleeping there so peacefully. He'd be right back, and she needed her rest.

Lizzie felt like she'd been out for an eternity. She heard the shower running and rolled over to check the clock. Almost nine. She'd been knocked out over twelve hours. Her body needed it. She slid up in the bed, recalling last night. It had obviously been Kyle's first time, hardly earthshattering, but there had been something so sweet and vulnerable about him, something that made her want to protect him and take that hurt away, which made the moment special. She knew what she'd said yesterday cut him. As much as he tried to stick his chest out, he was just a scared kid, in way over his head. Not that she wasn't.

The way he reacted to the obvious, she knew on some level

he must've suspected the truth, but it's so much easier not to look at those parts. She couldn't imagine how hard that had to be. Losing a mom so young. A father who was not around and still managed to disappoint. She could understand why his dad did it. We all want to impress with more than what we are. Not that that made it right. He'd fed Kyle a line of bullshit his entire life. Why hadn't his cousin figured it out?

Kyle came out of the bathroom in jeans, scrubbing the tangled mass of black hair, his body long and lean. He would grow into a handsome man one day.

"Hey," he said, trying to sound cool, but his cheeks flushed pink, and she knew he was picturing her naked on top of him. "You sleep like a rock." He pulled the tee shirt over his head and checked the bedside clock. "I was about to wake you up."

She let the sheet fall. She couldn't help it; she loved the reaction. "We have the room till eleven."

He looked away, toward the window. "I thought we could get some breakfast across the street."

"What's the hurry?"

"Nothing," he said, trying not to stare. "Out of cigarettes." He made for the handle. "I'm going to grab another pack. Meet me across the street in ten." Kyle bolted out the door.

What the hell? Maybe Lizzie didn't understand guys as much as she thought she did.

Kyle's heart jammed in his throat. Jesus. How could the sight of a naked girl do that to someone? But he didn't want her to be late, and he couldn't afford to stick around.

Several motels like the Tropicana lined the strip. Tourists and beach bums strode up and down the boulevard, homeless trundling shopping carts, street kids like Raf toting skateboards, kicking out tricks when the moment was right. He would've preferred a proper goodbye. Maybe he'd get another chance.

Kyle climbed the back steps to a neighboring motel, found

the stairwell with roof access, perched himself behind an industrial air conditioner, and waited.

Fifteen minutes later, he saw Lizzie cross the street to the restaurant parking lot. A man got out of his car, approaching fast. She stopped, taking in what was happening. Then she ran to him and threw her arms around her dad.

Kyle had finally done something good. He wished he could've walked her across, but she never would've let him go.

Mr. Decker had been cool on the phone. Kyle was worried he would blame him. But he said he just wanted his daughter home safe and wasn't accusatory at all. Before Kyle even explained his side of the story, Mr. Decker was agreeing with him. Kyle gave him the restaurant address and picked a time they'd be there, and Mr. Decker said he was on his way. He told Kyle to turn himself in before this went any further. Kyle said they could talk about it tomorrow. He had no intention of doing that. He'd been at the Skunk Train with Deke and Jimmy, and people had died, including cops. Kyle was the only one left. He didn't tell Lizzie's father any of this. Mr. Decker kept thanking him, as if Kyle was some dangerous thug and not a kid trying to do the right thing. Kyle asked him not to call the cops until after he picked up his daughter. Mr. Decker promised he wouldn't.

Then the squad cars pull in.

CHAPTER THIRTY-ONE

In the Apricot Family Restaurant parking lot, Lizzie sat on the bumper of an ambulance, which the cops had insisted on calling, despite her telling them that she was fine. They were treating her like the victim of a horrible kidnapping. They had Kyle all wrong. The police bandied about terms like "situation" and "dangerous," making Kyle sound like an unhinged lunatic.

The paramedics wrapped her in a blanket and a nice uniformed policewoman brought her an iced coffee and a muffin. The authorities were talking to her dad. A few days ago, they had him in handcuffs, and now they wanted his take on something he had nothing to do with. Every time she tried to set them straight, she was shooed back to the ambulance and told to wait for the detective in charge.

Cars, motorcycles, and buses barreled along Sunset Boulevard, making it difficult to tell what was happening across the street, where police had descended, scoping out their hotel room. She heard a cop report back that Kyle was not inside. She could've told them that.

Her father returned with two men in suits, leaving behind a well-dressed, serious-looking Asian woman, who corralled additional officers, directing them up and down the strip to the other hotels and eateries, even rooftops, like a squadron of helicopters was about to dip down from the sky and conduct a full-on fugitive search.

"This is Detective Jacobs," her father said. "From up north, where your friend Kyle lives."

"How are you holding up, Lizzie?"

This guy was a cop? With his bright blue eyes and flawless features, he looked more like a movie star than a detective.

"And this," Jacobs said, "is Detective Snelling with the LAPD. Old friend of mine."

The way Snelling's face soured when Jacobs said that told Lizzie the men were not friends.

"When was the last time you saw the suspect?" Snelling asked.

"Suspect? Suspected of what?"

"Lizzie, please," her father implored.

"I tried to tell you, Kyle didn't take me against my will. I don't know where you got this idea."

"Melanie called—"

"Melanie escaped out the window, and left me to fend for myself with that psychopath—"

"Psychopath?"

"Not Kyle. Jimmy."

"James McDermott," Jacobs said to Snelling. "Your DOA at the Royal Hotel. He was involved in the shootout at the Skunk Train."

"Did this Jimmy hurt you?" her father asked.

"No."

"And you're sure Kyle didn't—"

"Jesus!" Lizzie shouted loud enough to turn heads.

Jacobs turned to Dave Decker. "Would it be all right if I spoke with Lizzie in private?"

"I think I should be there if you're talking to my daughter."

"It'll be fine." Jacobs winked. "Promise."

"Yes, please," Lizzie said. "Go call Mom."

Jacobs tapped Lizzie on the shoulder. "You up for taking a walk?" He held up a hand for Snelling not to follow. "Let me take this one, Jack. Old time's sake."

Jacobs walked with Lizzie through the throng of EMTs and police.

"Looked like you could use a break from your dad." He had a warm smile and kind eyes.

"I know he means well, but I wish someone would listen to me."

"I'm listening."

"Kyle didn't kidnap me. I *offered* to help."

"Help do what?"

"At first he said he needed to get his truck out because it had all his money."

"Jim McDermott's truck and stolen money."

"Yeah, but—"

"Did Kyle tell you how he came in possession of that money?"

"Sort of. He said his cousin and Jimmy found a bunch of pot—"

"They stole marijuana. A great deal of marijuana. Almost a hundred pounds. Which belonged to the Sandoval Cartel. Do you know who they are?"

Lizzie shook her head.

"Nobody you want to steal from."

"But Kyle didn't do anything. His cousin stole it, and he and Jimmy were the ones who tried to sell it."

"To an undercover officer."

"I think they were going to kill us."

"Who?"

"The two cops who threw us in their car. Carter and Banks. They shot Jimmy. Didn't tell him to put his hands up or freeze or anything."

Jacobs rubbed the back of his neck.

"I'm telling the truth. They weren't regular cops." She leaned in. "Jimmy said they were dirty."

"Jim McDermott. The career criminal." Jacobs wrinkled his mouth. "That's a serious allegation, Lizzie. But I appreciate you telling me. I promise, I'll look into it." He shook his head. "This whole ordeal is getting out of control, wouldn't you say?"

Lizzie nodded.

"Which is why I need to speak with Kyle. Alone. It's imperative you tell me where he is."

"He's not dangerous."

"You know that, and I know that." Jacobs pointed at the legions of cops, letting his gaze linger on the stern Asian woman detective. "Some people have their own agendas."

"Kyle doesn't know anything."

"Let me decide that. It's my job. I'm on your side here. You have to trust me. When cops die, temperatures rise and tempers get short. Now do you have any idea where Kyle might be going?"

"Try and find his dad."

"Do you have an address?"

"We went to his uncle's yesterday to get it but he wasn't home."

"Where's his uncle live?"

She told Jacobs the address. "But you're wasting your time. His wife didn't even know he had a brother."

The Asian detective began to cross the street, directing several officers to fan out.

Jacobs stepped toward the road. "Hold on," he hollered, waving everyone back.

"We're going to search the surrounding properties," the woman detective shouted above the din of whizzing traffic. "He couldn't have gotten far."

"Not necessary," Jacobs said. "New information." Then he turned around and bent down to Lizzie. "Let's keep what you told me between us, okay?"

Kyle observed the whole scene from the rooftop of the hotel next door, opening and closing the Swiss army knife Deke had given him, certain the jig was up. He couldn't keep his hands from shaking and feeling like he was flying off the rails, which was what happened every time he got overwhelmed, like a thousand impulses fired inside his synapses and his brain might fry from overload. Did everyone feel like this? Once, after a bad fight at school, when he'd lost his temper, a teacher called him crazy. In moments like this, when emotions jerked him in fifty different directions, he couldn't help but wonder if she was right.

Why did he pick the hotel right next door? He was trapped. The only way off the roof was down the stairs, which ran along the side of the building, in plain view of everyone below. He'd almost believed Mr. Decker that there was a way out of this. You don't send out the cavalry to ask a couple questions. He was as guilty as Jimmy and Deke as far as the police were concerned.

He peered over the air conditioner and could see Lizzie talking to a man in a suit. A team of cops began crossing the street, heading straight for him. Kyle ducked behind the bulky unit, took a deep breath, clutched the knife tighter, steeling himself. But when he peered around the edge again, all the officers were getting in their squad cars and leaving.

A few moments later, Mr. Decker and Lizzie climbed into his SUV, the detectives their sedans. And like that, it was over.

He looked down at the little knife quivering in his hand. Who was he kidding?

This had gone too far. He might've come within minutes of getting shot, dying like Deke. He had to turn himself in, deal with the consequences, whatever they were.

But first there was something he needed to do.

CHAPTER THIRTY-TWO

Stepping off the bus in front of Little Joy, Kyle couldn't shake the feeling he was being set up. He checked the back seats of parked cars, peeked between buildings, scoping the scene for open windows, cable trucks or suspicious delivery vans. But no one was climbing telephone poles with a pair of binoculars. Two drunks with paper bags sat outside the bar, and scraggly cats prowled in piles of rubbish. Was he imagining the whole thing? Maybe no one was looking for him. He was a sixteen-year-old kid who didn't matter after all, a thought that both relieved and depressed him.

Please let his uncle be home. After all he'd gone through these past few days, he deserved the truth.

This time when he knocked, a man answered. Rail thin, with hollow, puckered cheeks and gray stubble, he reeked of alcohol despite the morning hour. His languid eyes seemed more annoyed than surprised. Kyle had no recollection of ever meeting his uncle, yet there was a vague familiarity about him.

"What do you want?"

"Who is it this time?" a woman shouted as a TV blared and baby bawled.

"No one," the man shouted. "A neighborhood kid looking for his lost dog." The man shooed Kyle off the porch and followed him outside, turning over his shoulder. "I'm going to the store for smokes."

"We need milk. And diapers. And wipes—"

The man whisked Kyle away from the house, walking with him around the corner. He stopped to light a smoke.

Kyle stared until the man offered him the pack. Kyle shook him off.

"Let's take a walk," Joe Kelly said, stopping before the entrance to Little Joy and pointing across the street. "On the other side.

The hot L.A. sun beat down. Big, linked buses exhaled hydraulics. Spanish hip-hop boomed out the backs of jacked-up low riders parked in front of a hamburger stand.

"I need to make a phone call," Joe said. "No fucking pay phones in this city anymore."

Kyle followed as he turned left down West Sunset.

"Deke tell you where to find me? We had a deal he wasn't going to do that."

Kyle didn't like this man, and he could see why Deke didn't want anything to do with him either.

"I couldn't care less about you. I want to find my father. Why'd that woman back there say you don't have a nephew?"

Joe stopped and spun around, but didn't answer the question. He didn't have to. The look in his eyes told Kyle everything.

Joe Kelly plowed ahead, past laundromats and discount tobacco shacks, like he was pissed off just to be awake, just to be alive, for having been born.

There was a pay phone in front of the liquor store. "Hold on," he grumbled, grabbing the receiver and pointing at the door. "Wait over there."

A sinking feeling took hold of Kyle's gut. This was what he'd been searching for? His big plan for the future, the ace he thought made him special? In that moment he wished more than anything he had picked up that gun in the back seat of the cop car. He yearned to clamp his mouth around a barrel, bite down hard, and pull the trigger.

As soon as his father hung up the phone, that feeling passed, replaced by something deeper, stronger, more primal, an instinct to survive.

"You can't be coming around," Joe said. "I got a new life now. New wife, kid."

"I thought you made movies?"

"Movies? Who the hell told you that?"

"Your letters."

"I never sent you any letters. I ain't heard a word about you since the funeral." Joe scanned the street, then waved Kyle to follow him inside the liquor store.

"I can't answer any of this for you, kid," Joe said as he passed the dairy case, heading straight for the beer, grabbing a six-pack from the bottom rung, the cheap stuff. "You need to ask your brother."

"My brother?"

"Deke wanted you to stay with him. His idea." At the counter, Joe pulled out a couple creased bills and a fistful of change. "Pack of GPCs," he said to the clerk.

"Deke is dead."

Joe glanced over at Kyle, disaffected.

"Eleven thirty-seven," the clerk said.

"GPC *Lights*." Joe pushed back the wrong pack of cigarettes.

Kyle glowered at him.

"Don't look at me like that. You're what? Fourteen?"

"Sixteen."

"Make it to forty-nine and tell me how much of your idealism you have left." He grabbed his brown sack and stalked out, taking a seat on the sidewalk and cracking a beer. Joe nodded at the concrete beside him.

Kyle didn't move.

"Suit yourself."

Kyle stared down at this stranger with the bald spot and bad posture, this mouthbreather hunched over like a disgruntled ape. How had he made this man the solution to all his problems?

"I wasn't cut out for fatherhood," Joe said, packing the new smokes. "Joan—" He peered over his shoulder. "That was Deke's mother. She did a number on me. Christ, I loved her. You get one chance to fall in love, kid. That first time. That's it. After that, they start chipping away until there's nothing left of your black heart." He cracked a tab and took a swill of beer. "Your mother and me, we weren't supposed to be together. Deke and me, we never got along. Even when he was a little boy. He blamed me for a lot of shit. Said you should live with him. And that was that. He didn't want me having any contact with you, and truth is, I had no interest. No offense."

Kyle now knew why Deke had done everything he'd done, a revelation that made his heart break.

"Good to see you turned out okay," Joe said. "Don't contact me again."

"Turned out okay? You have any idea what I've been through trying to find you? Of course you don't. I see why Deke hated you."

Joe stood and opened his mouth like he might have something more to say, but he didn't. Instead, he walked away, through the liquor store parking lot, as the dark blue sedan pulled in, stopping in front of Kyle.

A man got out. He held a badge in his hand. "Hello, Kyle." He thumbed toward the back seat. "Let's take a ride."

CHAPTER THIRTY-THREE

The man introduced himself as Detective Jacobs from Cutting. He said a lot of folks had been worried about Kyle since the shootout at the Skunk Train. But it was all going to be okay now. These words should've calmed Kyle, but they didn't. Meeting his dad, having invested so much time in a lie, left him reeling and numb.

"Your girlfriend's concerned about you."

"She's not my girlfriend."

"Could've fooled me." Jacobs waited to take a left through a busy intersection, light lingering on green but opposing traffic unwilling to take a break. "You would've saved yourself—and her—a lot of trouble if you'd come in after the Skunk Train. With the money."

"I didn't meet Lizzie until I got to San Francisco." Kyle watched the used hubcap shops, convenience stores, and taquerias zip by. The apartments and projects spread out farther and farther, until the neighborhoods dried up.

They caught the interstate. Kyle could feel Jacobs watching him in the mirror.

"Why don't you start by telling me about the dope. How'd you get your hands on it?"

"That was Deke and Jimmy."

"They tell you who the buyer was?"

Kyle caught his eyes in the rearview.

"You get a look at him?"

"Who?"

"The buyer. At the Skunk Train."

Jacobs crossed two lanes of traffic and exited the freeway, whipping the car around a loop and depositing them in a desolate industrial section under the bridge. Long, gray tankers and grounded shipping containers lined the side of the access road, rusted, hollowed out, abandoned to the elements.

A giant water tower speared the sky.

"I didn't see anything," Kyle said. "I was in the motel room."

The surroundings grew bleaker. Empty factories perched beyond concrete ravines, spray-painted with graffiti screeds. Off in the distance, planes disappeared into the washed-out blue. No one on the streets, no one peeped out windows, most of the storefronts vacant, boarded up, deserted. Somehow they'd landed in a ghost town in the middle of the biggest city on the West Coast.

"Where are you taking me?"

Jacobs didn't respond to the question, instead carrying on his own conversation. "I wish I could believe that. Would make my life a lot easier."

Jacobs veered down a narrow, unpaved road, curling behind a crumbling brick building. He stopped and set the car in park. He reached over to the glove compartment, flipped it open, pulled a pen from his breast pocket and stuck it through the finger guard of a gun. He lifted the revolver out, and with a handkerchief tucked the piece away in his coat pocket.

He turned over his shoulder. "I hope you understand, this isn't personal. It's the last thing I feel like doing, but I can't take any chances."

Kyle's eyes grew wide as the realization sank in.

"You?" Kyle said. "You were the third man at the Skunk Train."

"Calm down, kid. It's gonna be okay." Jacobs pinched the bridge of his nose and shook his head, as if trying to dislodge some unpleasant thoughts stuck inside. "Fuck," he muttered, then kicked open the door and hauled Kyle from the back seat.

Up ahead, a hollowed-out warehouse waited, fire scorched and ravaged. Rivered vines slithered through the fissures. A dingy sign hung askew from steel links. A picture of a cow. Some kind of meatpacking plant, the lingering stench of slaughter steeped deep into stone. Kyle tried to fight back, stumbling on the loose gravel, which made Jacobs jerk harder.

"You can't do this," Kyle said. "My...father...saw you pick me up."

"Who do you think he was calling at the liquor store?" Jacobs dropped him in the dust. He pulled a cell phone and held it up. "Fifty dollars and that drunk isn't remembering anything. Believe me, kid, I've spent the last few days winding everyone tighter'n a drum over your mental state."

Kyle pitched back on his elbows, leering up at Jacobs.

"Your cousin was your brother? Your uncle your father? Who gives a shit? But the story I've spun, no one's going to be surprised. That's if they ever find your body." Jacobs refastened his grip around Kyle's collar.

Kyle knew if Jacobs got him inside that warehouse, the fight was over. He'd shoot him between the eyes like Carter and Banks did Jimmy. He clutched at crabgrass and twigs poking through the hard clay, anything to gain traction, but he couldn't find root.

"When I realized that backpack wasn't in the car," Jacobs said, without breaking stride. "I doubled back, but by then the truck was gone. All I could do was hope I got the call to clean up the mess."

Like he was baling hay, Jacobs pitched Kyle across the threshold, headlong into the dark slaughterhouse. Broken glass from shattered windows sliced Kyle's arms and back, his head smacking against a giant pot-bellied stove. Up above, pipe arms twisted from its guts. Taut cables with huge hooks dangled from a conveyor belt.

"You had to go on this trip to find your daddy. I don't get it. Troubled boys and their daddies. Wasn't like that when I was a kid. Fuck, my father never said he loved me his whole rotten life. Look at me. I turned out fine. I could've handled this up in Dormundt, pain free. But you had to turn this into a goddamn adventure. Carter and Banks were supposed to have that money back in evidence. Was supposed to be wham bam. But you three dipshits had to fuck everything up. You know what a detective makes in Cutting? Thirty thou. Risk our lives all year long to put away dope dealers who make that in an hour." Jacobs wasn't even talking to Kyle anymore, more like he was carrying on an internal monologue, speaking into the ether and trying to convince himself. "Banish me from L.A. for that fuckhole?" He rubbed his eyes with the back of his hand.

"Doesn't matter if you kill me. The Mexicans took the money. I saw them."

"Wake up. How do you think they found you guys? They get their money back, Carter and Banks are out of the picture, I'm in the clear. You and your girlfriend should be history, too. But the fucking Mexicans. They got this bullshit code about women and children." It was meant as a declaration but came across more like a plea. "Someone has to take the fall. I can't leave any witnesses. You think I *want* to do this to a boy your age? This is going to haunt me for the rest of my life." He pointed his gun at Kyle. "Stand up."

"Why? If you're going to shoot me, what do you care where I am?"

Jacobs lurched forward, grabbing him by the scruff and hoisting him to his feet. Kyle reached around, hand sweeping air, searching for anything to hold onto or use as a weapon. When his hand brushed his back pocket, he remembered the Swiss army knife Deke had given him.

"What the fuck—" Jacobs turned toward the road.

The hollow, distant sound of tires speeding over gravel raced up the driveway, followed by the unmistakable pitch of squad car sirens.

Kyle had gotten out the pocketknife, fumbling to extend any sharp accessory. When Jacobs spun around, Kyle jammed the knife—or maybe it was the nail file or scissors—deep as he could into his thigh, twisting it like a fork twirling spaghetti. The detective screamed and clasped both hands to pull it out but the bent metal wrenched firmly in place. Kyle dove behind the pot-bellied stove as the detective took aim, firing wide. Kyle covered his ears and curled into a ball as stray bullets ricocheted off steel drums.

Commands from outside rose above the reverb. There was a loud boom, followed by a series of quick pings, as if from air rifles perched high in country hills. Then a groan and a crash, and footsteps raced toward him.

Kyle peered around the edge of the stove, and was met by Jacob's lifeless gaze, the Swiss army knife still embedded in his leg.

An Asian woman holstered her gun, stopping in front of him. "It's okay, Kyle. You can come out now. It's over."

At a downtown Los Angeles precinct, Kyle recounted the events of the last few days. He held nothing back, too exhausted to filter information. From Deke and the dope, to Raf and the perverts, to Lizzie and Monterey and Jimmy, the Greyhound ride and Skid Row, saying goodbye from the hotel rooftop, meeting his father, finding out he'd had a brother all along. The longer he talked, as painful as it was, especially the parts about Deke, the better he felt. So much had been bottled inside and pushed down for so long that spilling these feelings proved cathartic. Even though he was telling them more than they needed to hear, they let him talk.

Winos and junkies paraded past the desk where a police officer jotted pertinent information and the nice lady detective, Nomura, sat beside him. Even with the bars behind them and the locked-away lives, this was the safest Kyle had felt in a long time. He wasn't in trouble, Nomura said. He was the victim here.

Lizzie was on her way back to San Francisco with her dad.

They'd already relayed the message he was safe. Detective Nomura told Kyle how lucky he was Lizzie contacted her. It didn't sit right with Lizzie that a cop would want the information she shared with Jacobs kept secret. Nomura had been suspicious of Jacobs since her friend at internal affairs relayed the trouble her new partner had in L.A., which was why he'd transferred north. Carter and Banks came with their own tarnished reputations. Water seeks its own level. If Richter had been called in to investigate the Skunk Train murders instead of Cutting, Jacobs would've been the one on the run. Didn't matter, Nomura said: they were all cockroaches scurrying to escape the light.

The whole situation seemed surreal to Kyle, like something he might've once fantasized about, a film his make-believe father directed. Except the real-life version wasn't as alluring.

Afterward, Kyle was brought to a quiet room with a desk and chair. Nomura asked if he was hungry. Kyle nodded, and she left to get him something to eat.

Kyle sat in the chair. A few days ago, he'd been cutting class and hiding out behind the strip mall; today he was in an L.A. police station, and his life would never be the same. And the weird part was, that might not be a bad thing.

When Detective Nomura returned with a sandwich and soda, she set them on the table, and asked if he had any questions.

"What now?"

"You go home."

"I don't have one."

"Your brother's ex-girlfriend, Kristy, is on her way down to pick you up." The detective reached out and squeezed his shoulder. "You're going to be okay, Kyle."

She turned to leave. "Can I get you anything else while you wait?"

Kyle thought a moment. "You have any books?"

"Books?"

"Yeah, like, to read?"

The detective smiled. "I'll see what I can find."

LAST CHAPTER

The big truck rumbled to a stop in front of the house, the sodden smell of redwood creeping through the open windows. Kyle collected his books and the groceries he'd picked up after school and headed inside, where Kristy had already started to make dinner. Her school let out an hour earlier, and being closer to Dormundt, she always beat him home.

"You get the diced tomatoes and garlic?"

Kyle passed along the sack and opened the fridge, pulling out the quart of milk and pouring a tall glass.

"How'd it go today?"

He leaned against the counter. "I think I did fine."

"Fine?"

"All right. I nailed it."

It hadn't been easy getting caught up to speed after having missed so many classes, but everyone felt sorry for him after his ordeal, and Kyle worked hard to make the most of his second chance. He didn't ditch, didn't get in fights or cause any trouble. He read the assignments and participated in group discussions. Teachers noted the change in him. He didn't even need summer school.

Junior year was off to a great start. Classmates took the few details they had to weave a far more fantastic story. This latest version had Kyle kidnapped by a Mexican gang, escaping across the desert with some mysterious girl. He didn't bother correcting them. People were going to talk. And he couldn't have explained what happened out there anyway. It was more than learning the truth about his father, more than Deke, more than the Skunk Train, more than the violence and loss, even more than the girl. Wherever these things took him, the good and bad, in the end, they helped deliver him where he belonged.

The sweet smell of garlic sautéing filled the tiny kitchen. Kristy opened the tomatoes and added them to the sizzling frying pan.

"You going by the house?"

"Monday, after school. I have to try and fix that busted lock on the shed. Some kids must've tried prying it off again." Rumors persisted about giant stashes of pot hidden in the back shed. This was the third lock Kyle had to replace on his property. Everything that once belonged to his brother was now his.

Kyle thought of Deke often, tried to reconcile the memory he had of the hard ass always on his case with this new version of a brother who'd always been looking out for him. Even in death, Deke had set Kyle up with everything he needed to succeed, down to the small life insurance policy, which sat in Kristy's account until Kyle was ready to move into his house. Neither Kristy nor Kyle was ready for him to do that yet.

Kristy spilled out a plate of pasta and set it on the table. "Any plans for the weekend?"

"Thinking of heading down to San Francisco." He looked back over his shoulder. "If that's okay?"

"Isn't it every weekend?" she said with a grin.

Kristy switched on the iPod, piano intro fading in. Springsteen. Kyle and Kristy had a lot in common.

Out the window, evening fell as Kyle ate his dinner, staring into the dark spaces of the countryside. This was his home. Always had been. He only wished he'd seen it sooner.

Saturday morning, Kyle woke as the sun peeked over the mountains, buttery light spreading down the valley.

He climbed in his truck and fired the engine, fished out his latest mix CD from the center console. He popped the disc in the stereo and made for the freeway.

Kyle caught the onramp, heading south, and dug his cell from his jeans. He scrolled through his favorites, then checked the time. Still too early.

Before he got the phone back in his pocket, it rang. He smiled when he saw the name on the caller ID and reached over to turn down the radio.

"Hey," he said, "I was just about to call you."

ACKNOWLEDGMENTS

It's been a good few years in terms of books published. The 2nd edition to *Junkie Love*; the last of the Porter series; my first standalone with Down & Out Books. Also means I'm running out of ways to say thank you. So in addition to the usual suspects—my lovely wife, Justine; the boys, Holden and Jackson; and of course Tom Pitts—I just want to say thank you to everyone who reads my work. Knowing there are folks out there who are going to buy and read my new book, no questions asked, keeps me going on those dark doubting nights.

JOE CLIFFORD is the author of several books, including *The One That Got Away*, *Junkie Love*, and the Jay Porter Thriller Series, as well as editor of the anthologies *Trouble in the Heartland: Crime Fiction Inspired by the Songs of Bruce Springsteen*; *Just to Watch Them Die: Crime Fiction Inspired by the Songs of Johnny Cash*, and *Hard Sentences*, which he co-edited.

JoeClifford.com

On the following pages are a few
more great titles from the
Down & Out Books publishing family.

For a complete list of books and to
sign up for our newsletter,
go to DownAndOutBooks.com.

Forgiveness Dies
A Trevor Galloway Thriller
J.J. Hensley

Down & Out Books
October 2019
978-1-64396-038-8

Upon being released after being incarcerated in a psychiatric facility, former narcotics detective and unlicensed PI Trevor Galloway has no idea how to begin picking up the pieces of his shattered life.

When he's hired to investigate threats against a controversial presidential candidate and handed a stack of photos that may hold all the clues, he finds himself racing against time, running from mercenaries, and holding on to his last shred of sanity.

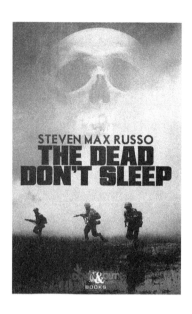

The Dead Don't Sleep
Steven Max Russo

Down & Out Books
November 2019
978-1-64396-051-7

Frank Thompson, a recent widower and aging Vietnam veteran, is down from Maine visiting his nephew in New Jersey. While at a trap range, they have a chance encounter with a strange man who claims to remember Frank from the Vietnam war.

Frank was part of a psychopathic squad of killers put together by the CIA and trained by Special Forces to cause death and mayhem during the war. That chance encounter has put three man on the squad on a collision course with the man who trained them to kill, in a nostalgic blood lust to hunt down and eliminate the professional soldier who led them all those years ago.

Pavement
Andrew Davie

All Due Respect, an imprint of
Down & Out Books
978-1-948235-99-0

McGill and Gropper are unlicensed private investigators who operate out of a diner and do whatever it takes to get a job done.

When a trucker attacks a prostitute, her pimp turns to McGill and Gropper for protection.

But taking the job means crossing dangerous and well-connected criminals who will stop at nothing to settle the score.

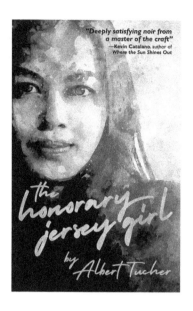

*"Deeply satisfying noir from
a master of the craft"*
—Kevin Catalano, author of
Where the Sun Shines Out

The Honorary Jersey Girl
Albert Tucher

Shotgun Honey, an imprint of
Down & Out Books
978-1-948235-10-5

Because sometimes she needs to get tough…

On the Big Island of Hawaii criminal lawyer Agnes Rodrigues hires an ex-prostitute turned bodyguard from New Jersey to protect an innocent man.

Two Jersey girls are tougher than one, even if one is honorary.

CPSIA information can be obtained
at www.ICGtesting.com
Printed in the USA
LVHW021702050120
642558LV00006B/822